International Influences and Inspirations in Education

Konrad Gunesch / Turhan Çetin (eds.)

International Influences and Inspirations in Education

PETER LANG

Berlin - Bruxelles - Chennai - Lausanne - New York - Oxford

Library of Congress Cataloging-in-Publication Data
A CIP catalog record for this book has been applied for at the Library of Congress.

Bibliographic information published by the Deutsche Nationalbibliothek. The German National Library lists this publication in the German National Bibliography; detailed bibliographic data is available on the Internet at http://dnb.d-nb.de.

ISBN 978-3-631-91924-8 (Print)
E-ISBN 978-3-631-91961-3 (E-PDF)
E-ISBN 978-3-631-92332-0 (EPUB)
DOI 10.3726/b22097

Published by Peter Lang GmbH, Berlin, Deutschland

info@peterlang.com - www.peterlang.com

This publication has been peer reviewed.

Konrad Gunesch

Turhan Cetin

Foreword: International Influences and Inspirations in Education, from Teaching and Learning over Expert Enterprise and Quality of Life, Up to Personal Transformation

The book you are holding in your hands, dear reader, has brought together noted experts in the field of education, in its generously defined and comprehensive sense of "universal teaching and learning, knowledge and appreciation". As such, it allows us to benefit from their accumulated and kindly shared experience, and from their theoretical and practical, financial and economic, mathematical and managerial, as well as cultural, linguistic and classroom viewpoints.

Such a wide and diverse array of perspectives is fortunately already the privilege and prerogative of "education" by definition, as it encompasses institutional and international, professional and personal, as well as formal and extracurricular insights, impressions and inspirations, and does so across subject areas, life stages, and public concerns. Education is also one among the very first sectors of society to receive and reflect worldwide technological progresses as much as terrifying pandemics, as we have all been working with or witnessed over the decisive span of recent years.

The nine chapters of this book have shouldered the formidable task of covering education within and across those eras, areas and aspects. They have achieved to do so with remarkable clarity and concision, insight and inspiration, by representing their specialized focus areas, while however pointing beyond themselves in their immediate implications and judiciously drawn conclusions.

I had the privilege and pleasure of experiencing these chapters just as you, dear reader, namely from perspectives of professional interest, pedagogical concern, and personal involvement, and by immersing myself in the respective research efforts, processes and results. But we have the luxury of not having to go through the considerable efforts that they had made to gather those results "in the field", or in close collaboration with their expert colleagues, or with students and teachers, or with other practitioners and educationally interested persons all around the world.

As we thus enjoy their finished products, we may only get a glimpse at the time and the patience it took to achieve them, such as when these experts' Methodology sections guide us, in objective, neutral and detached language, through the expanses of energies that they spent, so that we all, to use the famous expression of Sir Isaac Newton, can "see further by standing on the shoulders of giants". While our authors would probably not claim to be giants, they surely wish that we all can stand a bit higher, and can see a bit farther, after having immersed ourselves in their thoughts by following their chapters that they carefully divided into sections and headings of Introduction, Literature Review, Methodology, Empirical Investigation, Conclusions, and Recommendations.

Some of us might enjoy reading this book from cover to cover, convinced that all of its contents are of similar relevance and interest for them, even wishing that it contained many more chapters of its kind, and already anticipating the release of the next book of this type within the series. Others among us might pick and choose the chapters most interesting to them according to their current needs, or their professional backgrounds and personal preferences, or by following their temperament or the overall global tendency, such as when spotting contributions addressing the recent global pandemic, and taking this moment to reflect on some of the worldwide challenges and ongoing restructurings of education and economics, entrepreneurship and entertainment, and of other exciting and constantly evolving, international and interconnected aspects and areas.

As Classical Greek philosophy since Heraclitus has taught us that all things in life are constantly in a process of change, we expect the same from the topics and areas addressed in this book, all the more in the field of education, which is, among others, also defined by the perennial ideal and constant quest for human and social improvement. In that spirit, our journey of reading this book continues (or only properly starts) after these few lines of foreword, which are mostly meant to whet our reading appetites, warm up our critical minds and benevolent hearts, sharpen our discerning eyes and analytical dispositions, and humbly and helpfully offer to prepare us for discoveries through its chapters and contributions. Ideally, those will already in print and on paper support and inspire, enlighten and transform us, and allow us to grow together with the authors, or at least stand on their shoulders and be taller than we were just before our lecture.

Therefore, and without further ado, dear reader, I wish you a most educational and enterprising, enlightening and enlivening, exciting and entertaining, insightful and inspirational, but above all a transformative journey through this book. It has been one for me, since my very first reading, and it keeps being one even on renewed visits to these pages. Having now tried my best to make that reading journey palatable to you as well—if that was ever needed, given the chapter titles do evoke interest already at a first glance—I might even re-read a couple of these contributions together with you. Having done so professionally and academically as this book's editor has in any case opened to me one of the greatest privileges and pleasures of reading since the early days of books and print, namely that the journey, once completed, can restart at any moment that we choose, and each time from a higher and better perspective. Isaac Newton seems to have said it perfectly indeed, with those "shoulders of giants". Therefore, us reading the following pages now together, promises fresh peaks and panoramic perspectives for all of us, and each time we do so.

And with that thought, I gladly leave you to your own pace, process, and practice of immersion and enjoyment, as well as of professional growth and personal transformation. We might even meet again in a next book of this series—whether as readers, editors, or contributors, or maybe will do so one day in our professional lives, such as during conferences, or across classrooms. Whichever our points of departure and your lines of development, it is my honor and joy to walk a few steps of that journey of exploration together with you, during and in the service of our shared reflections on these readings. Please enjoy the lines, chapters and contents of this book, while I look forward to rejoining with you at the next step or intersection of our professional pathways, and across insights of disciplines, inspirations of development, or interactions of practice in our daily work, academic studies, or life endeavors, whether that will happen in person and on locations, or, just as interactively, intellectually along book lines and pages.

Contents

List of Contributors

Luisa Anderloni
University of Milan – Università degli Studi di Milano, Milan, Italy

Mislav Ante Omazić
University of Zagreb, Faculty of Economics and Business, Zagreb, Croatia

Fatlume Berisha
University of Prishtina "Hasan Prishtina", Faculty of Education, Prishtine, Kosovo

Sandra Cvetko
University North, Croatia

Zuzana Birknerová
University of Prešov in Prešov, Slovakia

Isabela-Anda Dragomir
"Nicolae Bălcescu" Land Forces Academy of Sibiu, Sibiu, Romania

Albane Fetiu
University of Prishtina "Hasan Prishtina", Faculty of Education, Prishtine, Kosovo

Anica Hunjet
University North, Croatia

Kerstin Knees
Palacky University of Olomouc, Czech Republic

Peteris Krasnikovs
RISEBA University of Applied Sciences, Latvia

Vjollca Markaj
University of Prishtina "Hasan Prishtina", Faculty of Education, Prishtine, Kosovo

Ornella Moro
University of Sassari – Università degli Studi di Sassari, Sassari, Italy

Brândușa-Oana Niculescu
"Nicolae Bălcescu" Land Forces Academy of Sibiu, Sibiu, Romania

Dagmara Ratnayake Kaščáková
University of Prešov in Prešov, Slovakia

Lucija Rutka
RISEBA University of Applied Sciences, Latvia

Martins Veide
RISEBA University of Applied Sciences, Latvia

Dijana Vuković
University North, Croatia

Maija Zakrizevska-Belogrudova
RISEBA University of Applied Sciences, Latvia

List of Figures and Graphs

List of Tables

Luisa Anderloni and Ornella Moro

Financial Literacy and Digital Literacy: Intertwined Issues of Increasing Importance

1. Introduction

The need to expand Financial Literacy (FL) has long been recognized and many studies and policy interventions by international organizations and national governments have addressed it. This is a consequence of the increasing complexity of financial products and transactions in various areas (payments, savings, financing and insurance) and, at the same time, of the increased financialization of the economy: nowadays many financial services are considered "universal services"[1], to which all citizens must have access to.

In recent times, this has been reinforced by the need to promote the digitalization of national systems and economies and, consequently, the general level of Digital Literacy (DL). Furthermore, the need to develop Financial Digital Literacy (FDL) also arises in light of the growing availability of online financial services and products.

A while back, the forerunner of digital services was called "home banking", and it was offered to customers with high financial availability who were interested in remote access to their accounts and investments for better management and faster transaction completion. Today the supply side (banks, financial, savings managers, and insurance), that in an effort to reduce costs and boost management efficiency, pushes towards digital financial relationships. But it penalizes traditional transactions conducted in person or over the counter with higher costs or even no service availability.

The concept of FL has been clearly defined by the OECD as a combination of knowledge, attitude and behavior (OECD-INFE, 2009). These elements are part of a wider wealth of knowledge, abilities and skills, behavioral conducts and habits of individuals. Their specific economic and financial components jointly contribute to determine financial literacy.

As for DL, it can be defined as the ability to access, manage, understand, integrate, communicate, evaluate and create information safely and appropriately through digital technologies for employment, decent jobs and entrepreneurship.

1 This research was funded by the University of Sassari (FAR—Fondo di Ateneo per la ricerca, 2019/University Research

It includes competencies that are variously referred to as computer literacy, ICT literacy, information literacy and media literacy (UNESCO, 2018). Indeed, the concept has evolved from a technical definition of skills and competencies to a broader comprehension including discernment, understanding and assess media messages to identify biases and evaluate messages independently.

There is a general acceptance of the above-mentioned definition of DL, with two additional specifications.

First of all, both the European Commission and the OECD—the two main organizations which in Europe actively deal with this issue—emphasize the role of DL for people's daily life, alongside with professional life and for empowering digital citizenship and social participation, in other words to promote the so-called "e-Inclusion" (European Commission, 2006; Buchholz et al., 2020).

Secondly, the risk not only of being the victim of unlawful conduct, but also of committing crimes or inappropriate behaviors by sharing files, texts, images and more, emphasizes the ethical issues, summarized in the proposed definition of DL in terms of the ability of individuals to interact on the basis of information "safely and appropriately".

Both FL and DL are a combination of knowledge, behavior and attitude: the latter in DL depends largely on the frequency of use. Digital financial literacy combines the skills needed to evaluate and properly use financial services with the skills to use digital technologies (Figure 1).

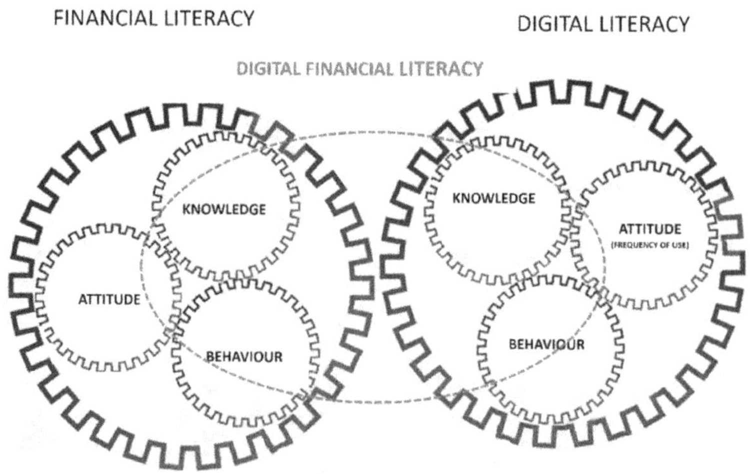

Figure 1: The components of FL, DL and FDL

There are broad similarities between the components of the FL and the DL: the geographical and personal determinants of individuals and outcomes are conceptualized and shown in Figure 2.

Alongside knowledge there are behavioral profiles that in the financial sphere can be summarized in impulsive purchases versus a rational habit to act on the basis of budgets. As regards the technological aspects of behavior, they are often linked to the frequency of use leading to confidence in understanding instructions and developing routines.

With regard to attitudes in the financial sphere, they refer to the willingness to think about the future and, therefore, to make investment choices by contrast to immediate consumption, in order to be able to face the uncertainties of the future and the needs in retirement age. In the digital field, they refer to the readiness to apply innovations, the patience to follow routine and instructions for use and the ability not to be discouraged in the face of difficulty in use or unforeseen operations.

Recently, the need for FL, on the one hand, and DL, and by extension DFL as a whole, has increased significantly due to two phenomena: the advent of fintech and the growing digitalization of the economy and society that has been accelerated by the COVID-19 pandemic.

In addition, the European Recovery and Resilience Facility represents a great opportunity for European countries to invest in digital transformation and actively promote conscious, safe and public use so that the benefits of technological innovation are fully exploited and the opportunities and threats opened by artificial intelligence are seized upon and tackled with.

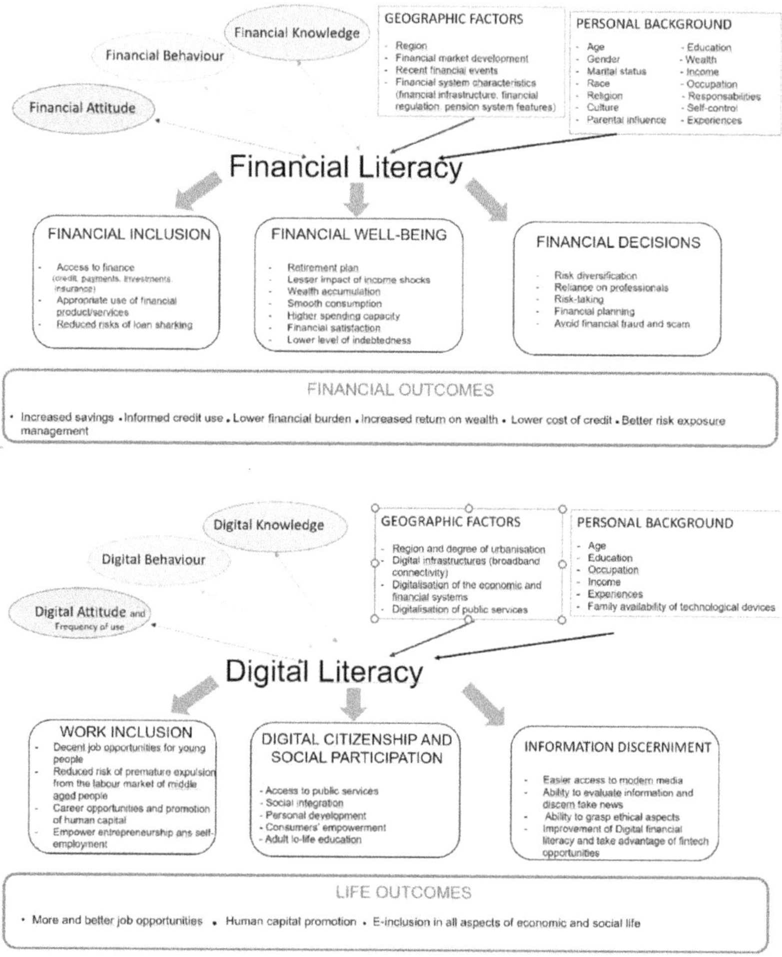

Figure 2: Determinants and outcomes of financial literacy and digital literacy

After this defining and conceptual introduction to FL, DL and DFL, the rest of the chapter is organized as follows. In paragraph 2 a short picture of the state of art in terms of FL and DL in European countries and their gaps is presented. In paragraph 3 a bibliometric content analysis on the two issues (FL and DL) and their links is proposed and in paragraph 4 the development trajectories of the initiatives at the international level are identified and a model of coordination of

FL initiatives that has proved to generate useful multiplier effects is presented. Paragraph 5 gives final remarks.

2. A Snapshot on Levels of Financial and Digital Literacy in Europe

The attention paid by international bodies to the promotion of FL and DL has led to the development of useful indicators to monitor the situation, the progress made and the existing gaps to be filled.

Considering the score proposed by Eurobarometer (2023) on FL as a whole, a picture of the situation is illustrated in Graph 1 where the vast majority of the different countries is on a medium level and marginally on low or high levels. In the case of DL, the distribution of the population in the different countries by literacy levels is more articulated, with levels frequently below the baseline levels and with sharp differences between countries as highlighted in Graph 2.

In the two fields there is a certain symmetry in the top position (high level of competence) and in the bottom one, while there is no direct correlation in general between the high level of FL and DL at European countries' levels. Monitoring the progress, the data also show that both levels of literacy are increasing slightly over time (Eurobarometer, 2023; European Commission, 2022).

However, major disparities still exist between Member States: this probably reflects the different "geographical" factors highlighted in the above Figure 2 which, alongside individual elements, contribute to determining literacy levels.

As Graph 3 well highlights, differences in levels across countries are more pronounced in the case of DL. This can be explained first, by the awareness developed over a longer period of the need to promote basic financial skills and the practice to encourage financial services providers to improve communication, contractual conditions and implement financial literacy initiatives for the benefit of customers and not included people (Anderloni & Moro, 2023a). Secondly, it can also be accounted for by a higher take up of digital technologies and their pervasiveness in social as well as working life. All these factors contribute to increasing the level of digital skills that are considered basic in today's social and working life.

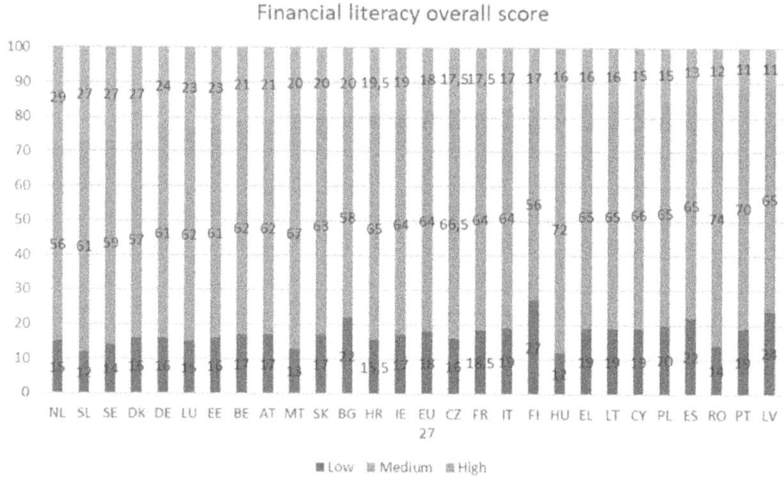

Graph 1: Financial literacy overall score 2023
Source: Elaborated from Eurostat data

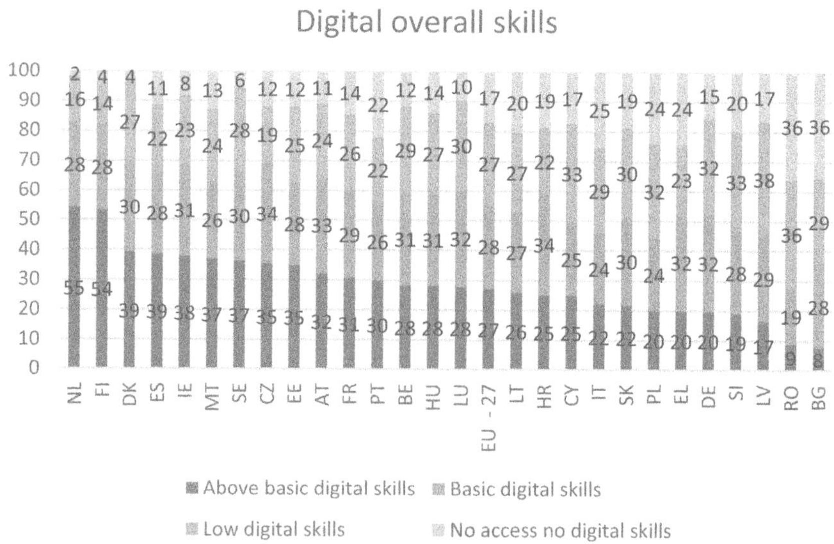

Graph 2: Digital overall skills 2023
Source: Elaborated from Eurostat data

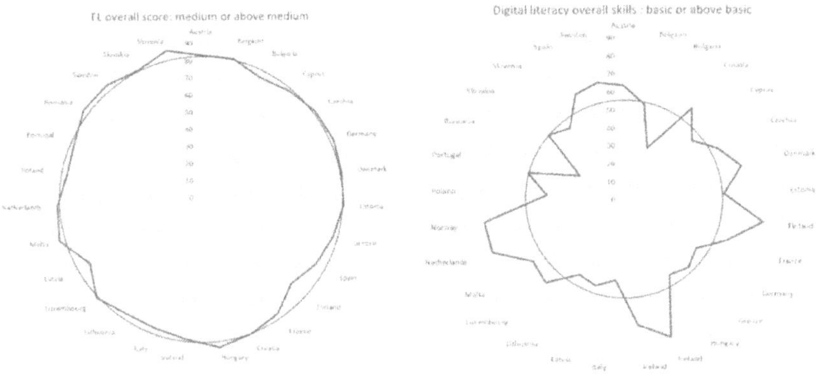

Graph 3: More than basic FL and DL: gaps among countries (in red the EU average-27 countries)

Source: Elaborated from 2023 Eurostat data

The importance of FL and DL in everyday life, as well as in working life and the negative effects of their deficiencies in particular in the most fragile segments of the population, in those of less educated and at risk of social marginalization, has raised the interest of both the scholars of different disciplines, and the policy makers of various levels that gave rise to numerous promotional initiatives with recommendations, guidelines, observers for monitoring, working groups and funding.

In the following paragraphs we present the literature approaches and the policy makers' suggested initiatives.

3. Content Analysis of Financial and Digital Literacy Literature

FL and DL have been studied in-depth independently (Anderloni & Moro, 2023b). But there are growing relations, direct or mediated between them and among them, and newly born variables/issues such as Digital Financial Literacy, Digital Economy, Digital Financial Inclusion, as Digitalization are increasingly affecting individuals' financial literacy and financial capability. The aim is our analysis is to investigate these relations.

3.1. The Methodology

To show these relations we used a bibliometric analysis: it is based on the use of keywords (occurrencies and co-occurrencies[2]) that are common proxies of the issues studied in a research field (Bedi et al. 2019 and Ding et al. 2019).

We used the Scopus database[3] to extract the list of publications coherent with our research goals. As spelling mistakes (singular/plural for the same terms, keywords with the same meaning but with a different synonym, etc.) affect the frequency of keywords co-occurrence, reducing the efficacy of the network map visualization, we made some minor adjustment on the thesaurus file. Before getting to the network visualization we excluded the overall present keyword "Financial literacy". We used Vosviewer software tool and we set at three the minimum number of keyword co-occurrence.

3.2 The Results

Our analysis allowed us to identify twelve clusters. A preliminary observation concerns the proximity or distance of different digital issues inside our map (see Graph 4).

2 In a Keyword Co-occurrence Networks (KCN) each keyword is represented as a node: the size of the nodes is proportional to the frequency of keyword occurrence (i.e., the number of times that the keyword occurs) (Ding et al., 2001).The link between the nodes represents the co-occurrence between keywords in different publications (i.e., keywords that co-occur or occur together). The thickness of the link identifies the occurrence of co-occurrences between keywords (i.e., the number of times that the keywords co-occur or occur together). The closeness of the nodes represents the interconnectedness between them.

3 We used Scopus database without defining limits to the time span, to the document types, to the language.

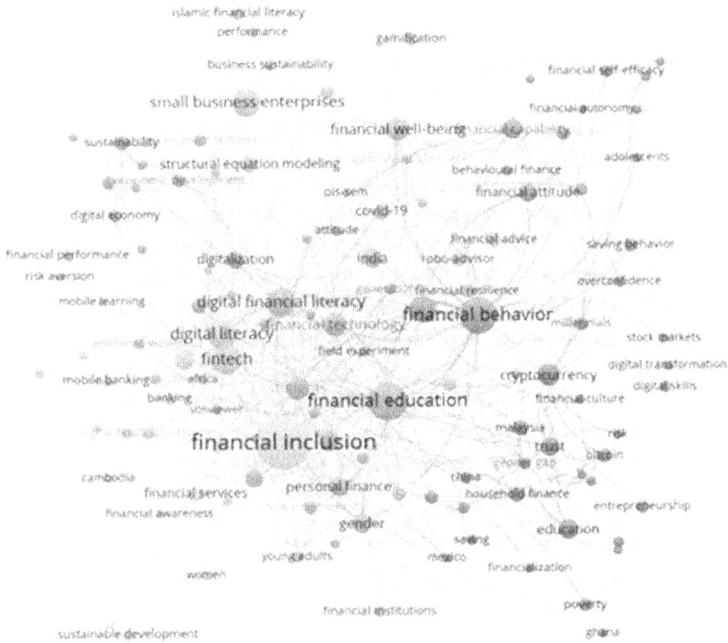

Graph 4: Clusters and nodes among financial literacy publications

Most nodes related to the digital world are widely scattered and pertain to different clusters but comes to light a strong closeness among issues such as Digital Literacy, Fintech, Digitalization and Digital financial literacy[4]: the surge in complex and innovative financial instruments, including peer-to-peer lending, cryptocurrency, digital wallets and robot-advisors and the predominance, for them, of digital devices and channels require DL and skills. At the same time, the higher consumers' digitalization, the greater the propensity to approach digital finance and fintech, given, of course, a minimum level of financial knowledge.

In the map there are clusters devoted to specific issues, such as the one relative to small business enterprises (light blue cluster) in which the only digital node included refers to digital payments, as this is the greatest interconnection to the

4 Also mobile payments, the yellow node whose label does not appear in the map, but also digitalization and digital payments.

digital world, given the growing diffusion of digital economy post the COVID-19 pandemic. This node has long distance links with other clusters' digital nodes (such as digital literacy, financial technology, digital financial services) as they are somehow connected with its evolution.

Another cluster includes financial education (dark green), in which digital nodes refer to digital technologies, information literacy, financial technology and digital finance. Given the fast development of digital financial services, financial education must necessarily include the skills, knowledge and issues linked to the digital world. For example, data vulnerabilities, the correct use of PINs and passwords, the detection of false websites are necessary competencies more often included in the initiatives of financial education. On the other hand, digital technologies can advance financial literacy and play a key role in financial education.

The light green cluster with financial inclusion as its main node is scarcely populated, but the node is the biggest in the map, due to a high frequency, and has the highest number of links to other keywords and to nodes of the digital world. The closer are information literacy, digital technology and then fintech, digital literacy and digital financial literacy. Digital technologies lower the cost of basic financial products/services, provide an entry point into the formal financial system, broaden and deepen access to new types of financial products, increasing in this way financial inclusion. But digital literacy and digital financial literacy are both required.

The red cluster is made of small nodes relative to households finance and themes, such as saving, investment, risk, and here, aside from the traditional themes of education, financial culture, financial literacy education appear issues related to bitcoin or cryptocurrency, together with trust.

The growing popularity of cryptocurrencies, despite its high risks, increases the need of skill and competencies both in term of digital literacy, for understanding its technicalities, and in terms of digital financial literacy, for a global assessment of the risks (which are higher than the price risks, due to the lack of regulators and supervisors).

Focusing on the specific node of digital literacy, apart from the already mentioned closeness to keywords such as digital financial literacy, fintech and financial technology, we note that there also are links with other keywords/issues of the digital world, such as artificial intelligence, information technology, mobile learning, digital financial inclusion, digital economy and links with issues specific of the financial literacy research area, such as financial inclusion, personal finance, financial skills.

For researchers on FL themes, it is important to understand both the potential of AI into the financial supply—with the impact of risk assessment models and the use of non-traditional data sources on financial products prices and on inclusion - and its limitations and risks, as low income individuals might access more convenient loans but risk falling into excess borrowing and unsustainable debt levels. The effect can be both positive and negative since limited access to digital skills and to technology as a protection might keep some people from fully benefiting from AI-powered financial services. AI gives customer access to simplified procedures to compare credit online offers and highlights relevant elements for credit scoring influencing their financial literacy.

The links among mobile learning and digital literacy (and Digital financial literacy) highlight the focus on the potentialities of this technological device in increasing knowledge and skills: mobile devices are used by a larger population than computers, the smartphones/tablets are connected to the internet world and also give access to a wide arena of apps, for mobile payments and banking but also for many other financial services. Mobile learning is connected to digital literacy by sharing many issues and it is a two way relation, and it is connected to digital financial literature as smartphones are increasingly used for payments and financial transactions.

In this digital era, FL is not sufficient for making good financial decisions. DL and DFL increase the ability to manage financial matters on digital platforms (Lyons & Kass-Hanna, 2021) and provide knowledge and tools to protect against digital fraud, thus increasing consumers' and SMEs financial well-being (Choung et al., 2023; Gosal & Nainggolan, 2023; Lankshear et al. 2008). Besides, DL, FL and DFL can influence the perception of a chance in one's financial well-being: the results of Rinadi and Strizzolo (2022) empirical research showed that DL helped protect against a worsening of one's economic situation.

In personal financial planning, digitalization can worsen financial well-being if investors without an adequate financial and digital knowledge easily access digital financial products. DL and FL should be considered together when assessing the implication of digitalization.

Other links which deserve to be mentioned are between SMEs and the digital economy: FL improves profitability of the firms concerned, but the combination of DL and FL improves also growth (Fauzi et al., 2020). In addition it influences, together with financial literacy, the financial behavior of the small entrepreneurs, that enhancing the impact of digital financial services (Angeles, 2022). FL and DL are instrumental in stimulating digital transaction behavior and enabling the digital economy.

Graph 5: Links among digital literacy and other issues among publications on financial literacy

DFL shares many links already discussed with DL, both relative to the digital world (fintech, artificial intelligence, financial technology, mobile learning, digital payments) and some specific of the financial literacy research area (financial inclusion, financial well-being, personal finance, financial skills). However, it is more related to an issue such as financial behavior: modern technologies and internet encourage risky behaviors and personal tendencies such as short-termism, impulse purchases, self-control problems. There is a consequent interest in the impact of DFL on resilience-building financial behaviors, including saving, borrowing, and risk management (Kass-Hanna et al., 2022; Varlamova et al., 2020; Setiawan et al. 2022).

Furthermore, of course, DFL is related to the issue of financial education: it is not enough for people to simply have access to digital financial services; they also need to understand how to use them to their advantage, both in terms of awareness of digital financial products, services and providers, in terms of technical confidence on devices and products/services, but also in terms of awareness of possible risky behaviors (buying before knowing how to use a digital financial product), and in terms of responsibilities and possible risks, in terms of knowledge of more intricate financial concepts (i.e. debt maturity, durations, payout options, etc.). Given the growing number of digital alternatives to traditional financial products and services and financial innovations spreading worldwide and the increased sophistication of financial markets, the relation between the two issues is important. There are also some practical issues concerning FL educational initiatives: if they are devoted to students and young people, there is a "natural" users' preference for a digital financial education linked to the understanding of critical concepts of financial literacy.

We already discussed the links between financial inclusion and artificial intelligence and these concepts also apply to DFL. Digital finance has made financial services more accessible, overcoming geographical barriers, and has boosted digital financial understanding: with a higher degree of digital financial literacy it is easier to engage in e-banking channels and digital financial services, increasing the level of digital financial inclusion and of financial inclusion itself.

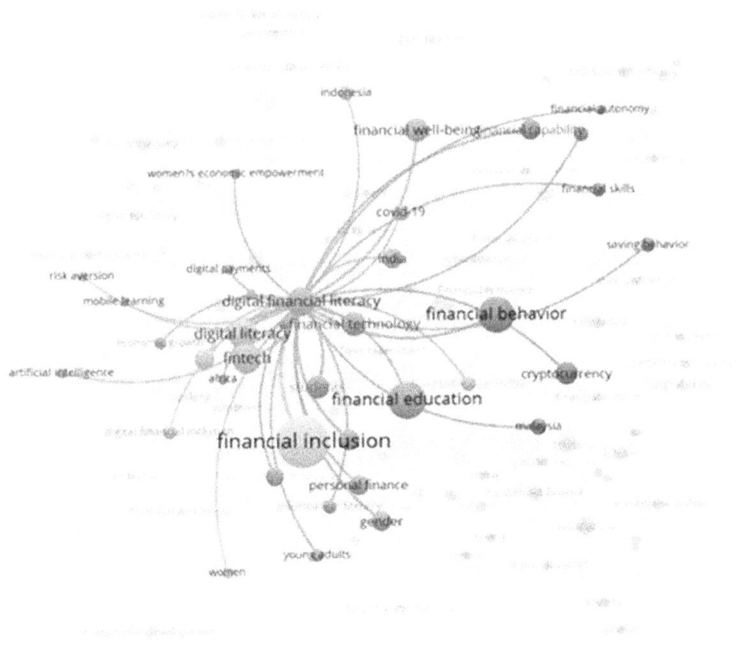

Graph 6: Links among digital financial literacy and other issues among publications on financial literacy

4. The Requirement for Multiplier Effects for Initiatives to Promote Financial and Digital Literacy

The main international players in the promotion of FL and DL are the World Bank, with specific reference to developing countries, the OECD[5] and the European Commission.

Within FL, supranational and national policy makers have also been able to use financial market regulation processes and policies to promote consumer protection. The purposes of promoting financial literacy have thus been intertwined with those of creating the single market in financial services, the creation of a European payment system and the establishment of the capital market union. This is accompanied by the objectives of raising awareness about the prevention of fraud, financial crimes such as money laundering and economically and socially harmful phenomena such as usury or over-indebtedness of households.

Targets of the interventions were young people, small entrepreneurs, self-employed adults or fragile adults in financial difficulties and at risk of marginalization.

Interlocutors and transmission belts for the implementation of the FL promotion policies have been multiple: regulatory and supervisory bodies, group associations (from the banking, financial and insurance sectors) on the one hand, and the micro and small business sectors on the other, the consumer associations and the voluntary associations closest to the needs of the fragile population.

The involvement of various ministries (Economy and finance, Education, Labor and Social Policy) also often plays an important role. Figure 3 schematizes the involvement of multiple subjects, as stated above, with reference to the Italian case

In the case of the DL, it should be noted that the interest from policy makers is more recent, but this topic has decidedly entered among the highest priorities on the European agenda. In fact, the DL is a corollary of digitalization that with green and sustainable development are the priority objectives for European policies: in the new strategic agenda 2019–2024 (European Council, 2018b) in order to develop a strong economic base digital transformation is a key factor. The EU commitment to promote digital transformation and guide artificial intelligence developments concerns infrastructure, connectivity, services, data,

5 See OECD (2009, 2016, 2017a, 2017b, 2018, 2020a, 2020b, 2021, 2022).

regulation and investment. Among investments those in people's skills and education are of utmost importance.

The European Commission, in setting its priorities for 2019–2024 gave high priority to climate change and the green economy as well as to digital transformation and people empowerment through a new generation of technologies (European Commission, 2018a). Digitalization is seen to bring multiple benefits to people in terms of creating new jobs, fostering new skills, developing new markets and enhancing the EU's competitiveness.

In parallel, under the EU commitment to providing young people with the best education and training (EU Rome declaration 2017), and the European Council call for training and education systems to be fit for the digital age (European Council, 2019), the European Commission promoted the digital education action plan (EU Commission, 2018a, 2018b) concerned with how education and training systems can make better use of innovation and digital technology and support the development of relevant digital competencies needed for life and work. It set out three priorities: (i) making better use of digital technology for teaching and learning; (ii) developing relevant digital competencies and skills for digital transformation and (iii) improving education through better data analysis and foresight. The plan has been updated in 2020 with the horizon 2021–2027 (EU Commission, 2020a, 2020b) and later with the Digital decade policy program 2030 (EU Commission, 2023a, 2023b). The latter highlights the need to accelerate and deepen the collective efforts to reach the goals through policy measures and investments in digital technologies, skills and infrastructures, in digitalization of business, in cybersecurity and resilience, and in monitoring the supply chain.

As for skills, the goal is to have at least 80 % of European population reaching (or over) basic digital skills. As Graphs 2 and 3 above have shown, the actual situation is still quite far from the goal and gaps are big.

Digital technology is seen to be both a study subject and a tool to improve results in education in various types and level of schools and lifelong education. In particular it can enable access to additional learning resources, support disadvantaged students (such as those from low socioeconomic backgrounds or with disabilities, or living in remote areas).

The "teaching teachers" model is widely used. In FL, initiatives often target specialist teachers (maths, economics or law) but in DL, unlike in FL, all teachers should be targeted because technologies are a useful support to every subject teaching and learning.

Furthermore, in order to reach a better positive impact and foster multiplier effects it is very important to stimulate a coordination of initiatives, involving actors of different nature (public, private and third sector), as in the Italian experience of FL. A Committee for planning and coordination of financial education activities was set up in 2017 with the mission of promoting and coordinating initiatives useful for raising financial, insurance and social security knowledge and skills among the population as to improve everyone's ability to make choices consistent with their own objectives and conditions (Anderloni & Moro, 2023a)[6]. It ensures the participation of competent ministries, regulatory and supervisory bodies, consumers and financial intermediaries' associations and plays an effective role in stimulating and coordinating a number of initiatives, as depicted in Figure 3.

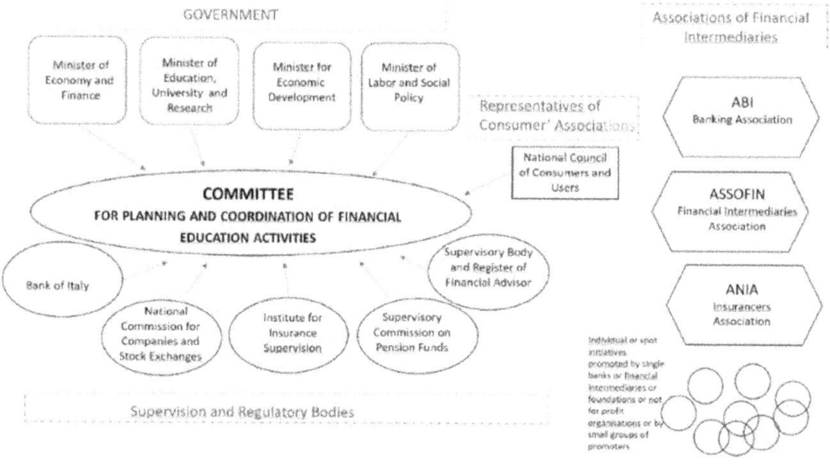

Figure 3: A coordination model of FL initiatives

5. Final Remarks

Today, young people are likely to be more self-confident in technology use and older people often more averse to using digital services. But in general, and

6 The coordination function is carried out, first of all, through the composition of the 11 members of the committee: they are designated by the competent minister, by the bodies of regulation and supervision over intermediaries and financial markets, by the National Council of Consumers and Users (CNCU), and the Supervisory Body and Financial Adviser Register (OCF).

in financial services in particular, competences tend to be overestimated and risks underestimated. The proliferation of high-tech or high-end digital devices, often with complex design or unfriendly user-interface issues may exacerbate difficulties.

Furthermore, it should be highlighted that mobile apps may not contribute to increasing users' digital literacy. They often only provide a quick and simplified way to access specific services with digital payments. The ease of use with only a few clicks may lead to involuntary purchases without sufficient evidence to enable corrections or claims. Chat boxes instead of enabling communication and anabling support often make it more difficult to have a direct relationship with the suppliers. As a consequence the consumers cannot really avail themselves of their rights.

There are also several risks associated with the mishandling of sensitive data and passwords associated with online financial services. Not all consumers take the necessary steps to safeguard their personal data online: for example, consumers are often unable to generate and remember PINs, they select simple number combinations, and write them down. Furthermore there are differences in perception of online security risks and few adopt strategies to minimize the likelihood of being victim of cybercrime.

Many consumers do not know or well understand the relevance of digital footprint when they share additional personal data with products and services providers, if this results in perceived benefits. Indeed, consumers may not be aware of the extent to which their data might be used: for instance they might be exposed to a wider collection of their personal data through "automated profiling", which enables businesses to discriminate, segment consumers into marketing categories, marginalize them as a result of opaque and potentially unfair data-mining practices, and exclude them from marketing opportunities.

There also are risks due to the effects of digital technologies on consumer behavior (inducement to compulsive spending) and on risk perception due to the customers' not understanding complex contracts or clauses. Lawfulness, fairness and transparency are often missing, and the rights to access, rectify or delete orders, are not adequately drawn attention to. To address these risks consumers must (at least) have a basic understanding of the obligations and potential issues associated with digital transactions.

For all these reasons, education is called to play a very important role, identifying the most effective tools to improve knowledge, behaviors and attitudes.

References

Anderloni, L., & Moro, O. (2023a). The needs for financial literacy in the fintech era. Italian experiences. In I. Maciula (Eds.), *Financial literacy in today's global market*. IntechOpen. Available at: http://dx.doi.org/10.5772/intechopen.1003808.

Anderloni, L., & Moro, O. (2023b). Content analysis of the financial literature over time in the world. In I. Maciula (Eds.), *Financial literacy in today's global market*. IntechOpen. Available at: http://dx.doi.org/10.5772/intechopen.1003705.

Angeles, I. (2022). The moderating effect of digital and financial literacy on the digital financial services and financial behavior of MSMEs. *Review of Economics and Finance*, 20, 505–515.

Bedi, H. S., Karn, A. K., Kaur, G. P., & Duggal, R. (2019). Financial literacy–a bibliometric analysis. *Our Heritage*, 67 (10), 1042–1054.

Buchholz, B. A., DeHart, J., & Moorman, G. (2020). Digital citizenship during a global pandemic: Moving beyond digital literacy. *Journal of Adolescent & Adult Literacy*, 64(1), 11–17.

Choung, Y., Chatterjee, S., & Pak, T. Y. (2023). Digital financial literacy and financial well-being. *Finance Research Letters*, 58 Part B. Available at: https://doi.org/10.1016/j.frl.2023.104438.

Ding, Y., Chowdhury, G., & Foo, S. (2001). Bibliometric cartography of information retrieval research by using co-word analysis. *Information Processing and Management*, 37(6), 817–842.

Eurobarometer. (2023). Monitoring the level of financial literacy in the EU. Report. *Flash Eurobarometer* 525, European Union.

European Commission. (2018a). *Communication from the Commission to the European Parliament, the Council, the European Economic and Social Committee of the Regions on the Digital education Action Plan, COM (2018) 22 final*, Brussels, January 17, 2018.

European Commission. (2018b). Commission staff working document. Accompanying the document European Commission *(2018a), SWD (2018), 12 final*, Brussels, January 17, 2018.

European Commission. (2020a). Digital education action plan 2021–2027. Resetting education and training for the digital age. Communication from the Commission to the European Parliament, the Council, the European Economic and Social Committee of the Regions, *COM (2020) 624 final*, Brussels, September 30, 2020.

European Commission. (2020b). Commission staff working document. Accompanying the document European Commission *(2020), SWD (2020), 209 final*, Brussels, September 30, 2020.

European Commission. (2022). Digital Economy and Society Index (DESI) 2022. *Thematic chapters*. https://digital-strategy.ec.europa.eu/en/policies/desi

European Commission. (2023a). Report on the state of the Digital Decade 2023. *Communication from the Commission to the European Parliament, the Council, the European Economic and Social Committee of the Regions*, COM (2023) 570 final, Brussels, September 27, 2023.

European Commission. (2023b). Commission staff working document. Accompanying the document European Commission *(2023a)*, SWD (2023), 573 final, Brussels, September 27, 2023.

European Union. (2006). Ministerial declaration. Approved unanimously on June 11, 2006, Riga, Latvia.

European Union. (2017). *Declaration of the leaders of 27 member states and of the European Council, the European Parliament and the European Commission*. Approved unanimously on March 25, 2017, Rome, Italy.

European Council. (2019), A New Strategic Agenda 2019–2024, https://www.consilium.europa.eu/media/39914/a-new-strategic-agenda-2019-2024.pdf

Fauzi, F., Antoni, D., & Suwarni, E. (2020). Women entrepreneurship in the developing country: The effects of financial and digital literacy on SMEs' growth. *Journal of Governance & Regulation*, 9(4), 106–115.

G20/OECD-INFE. (2018). Digitalisation and financial literacy.

Gosal, G. G., & Nainggolan, R. (2023). The influence of digital financial literacy on Indonesian SMEs' financial behavior and financial well-being. *International Journal of Professional Business Review*, 8(12). Available at: https://doi.org/10.26668/businessreview/2023.v8i12.4164.

Kass-Hanna, J., Lyons, A. C., & Liu, F. (2022). Building financial resilience through financial and digital literacy in South Asia and Sub-Saharan Africa. *Emerging Markets Review*, 51, Part A. Available at: https://doi.org/10.1016/j.ememar.2021.100846.

Lankshear, C., & Knobel, M. (2008). *Digital literacies: Concepts, policies and practices*. New York: Peter Lang. ISBN 978-1-4331-0169-4.

Lyons, A. C., & Kass-Hanna, J. (2021). A methodological overview to defining and measuring "digital" financial literacy. *Financial Planning Review*, 4(2). Available at: http://dx.doi.org/10.2139/ssrn.3836330.

OECD. (2016). *OECD/INFE international survey of adult financial literacy competencies*. Paris: OECD. www.oecd.org/finance/OECD-INFE-International-Survey-of-Adult-Financial-Literacy-Competencies.pdf

OECD. (2017a). *G20/OECD INFE report on adult financial literacy in G20 countries.*

OECD. (2017b). *G20/OECD INFE report on ensuring financial education and consumer protection for all in the digital age.*

OECD. (2018). *G20/OECD INFE policy guidance on digitalisation and financial literacy*. Paris: OECD.

OECD. (2020a). OECD/INFE 2020 international survey of adult financial literacy. www.oecd.org/financial/education/launchoftheoecdinfeglobalfinancialliteracysurveyreport.htm

OECD. (2020b). *PISA 2018 results (Volume IV): Are students smart about money?*. Paris: PISA, OECD Publishing, https://doi.org/10.1787/48ebd1ba-en.

OECD. (2021). *21st-century readers: Developing literacy skills in a digital world.* Paris: PISA, OECD Publishing, https://doi.org/10.1787/a83d84cb-en.

OECD. (2022). Evaluation of national strategies for financial literacy. https://www.oecd.org/financial/education/evaluation-of-national-strategies-for-financial-literacy.htm

OECD-INFE. (2009). *Financial education and the crisis. Policy paper and guidance.*

Rinaldi, E. E. & Strizzolo, N. (2022). Competenze digitali e finanziarie nel primo lockdown: l'impatto sul benessere finanziario degli anziani (Digital and financial skills in the first lockdown: The impact on the financial well-being of older adults). In *Salute e società*: XXI, 3, 4–63. Milano: Franco Angeli.

Setiawan, M., Effendi, N., Santoso, T., Dewi, V. I., & Sapulette, M. S. (2022). Digital financial literacy, current behavior of saving and spending and its future foresight. *Economics of Innovation and New Technology*, 31(4), 320–338.

UNESCO Institute for Statistics. (2018). *A global framework of reference on digital literacy skills for indicator 4.4.2.*

Varlamova, J., Larionova, N., & Kukushkina, O. (2020). How digital technologies affect consumers' financial behavior. In *Rivista internazionale di scienze sociali*: 3, 2020. Milano: Vita e Pensiero.

Isabela-Anda Dragomir and Brândușa-Oana Niculescu

Post-Covid Adaptations and Transformations in Teaching English as Foreign Language: Between the "New Normal" and the "Next Normal"

1. Introduction

In the aftermath of the global pandemic, the EFL (English as a Foreign Language) teaching landscape underwent a series of profound shifts, setting in motion a complex educational metamorphosis. What was initially dubbed as the "new normal"—characterized by digital integration, flexible learning environments, and revised pedagogical strategies—has progressively evolved into the "next normal". This transition signifies more than just an adaptation to unforeseen challenges; it encapsulates a forward-looking vision for education that is dynamic, inclusive, and resilient. The journey towards this "next normal" in EFL teaching underscores the sector's inherent capacity for innovation and reinvention. As we navigate this evolving terrain, it is clear that the lessons gleaned from our recent experiences are shaping a more holistic, student-centric, and globally interconnected EFL educational paradigm. The horizon beckons with opportunities to redefine language learning, ensuring it remains relevant, engaging, and attuned to the ever-changing needs of learners. As we embrace the "next normal", we are not merely adapting but actively charting the future of EFL education, exploring what lies ahead with optimism, purpose, and a commitment to excellence.

The onset of the COVID-19 pandemic created a domino effect across various sectors of EFL instruction, spanning from a re-adaptation of traditional teaching, learning and evaluation methods and techniques, to content and language as a tool for social exchange, and last, but not least, to the very nature of the educator-student relationship.

One of the most immediate transformations was the transition to online platforms. With the closure of educational institutions globally, there was an urgent need to continue the learning process. This led to a rapid shift to virtual platforms like Zoom, Google Classroom, and Microsoft Teams. The brick-and-mortar classroom, a staple of education for centuries, was suddenly supplanted by its digital counterpart.

This new format also mandated a modified curriculum and assessment. The traditional paradigms of EFL teaching and evaluation had to be rethought to suit the digital landscape. Instructors began devising innovative assessment methods, ranging from open-book examinations to digital portfolio presentations, to gauge student understanding in this new environment.

A consequential by-product of this digital transition was student autonomy and responsibility. The virtual setup naturally provided students with a greater degree of control over their learning trajectory. While this newfound independence empowered many, it also posed challenges, especially for those reliant on structured, physical learning environments.

However, educators soon realized the difficulty in replicating the traditional classroom dynamics online. The absence of physical presence demanded innovative strategies to engage students, manage virtual classroom behavior, and sustain active participation. Simultaneously, there was a discernible shift towards emphasizing soft skills. The unpredictability ushered in by the pandemic accentuated the importance of adaptability, resilience, and motivation, which became central themes in EFL curricula.

Central to all these changes was the reimagining of the role of teachers. No longer the sole disseminators of knowledge, educators transitioned to becoming facilitators. They were now tasked with guiding EFL students through a maze of resources, fostering an environment of self-directed learning and lending support where needed.

Despite its myriad challenges, the COVID-19 pandemic became a catalyst for transformation in the EFL domain and a driving force promoting educators' and students' resilience and adaptability.

2. Redefining EFL Pedagogy: Methodological Evolutions in the Post-COVID Landscape

With COVID-19 forcing schools and institutions to move instruction online, educators and learners were displaced from the physical classroom into the virtual one. This situation presented educators with both opportunities and challenges, not least of which was familiarizing themselves with technologies, adapting their courses to remote delivery, and maintaining continuity for their students. In order to provide high quality instruction in online learning, online course instructors had to reconsider the traditional set of beliefs about learning (Niculescu & Dragomir, 2021). Principles that used to be successful in the traditional classroom "must now be modified to facilitate effective online learning" (Richards et al., 2004, p.101). Research in this direction (Gacs et al.,

2020; Mavridi, 2022, 2023; Moser et al., 2021; Oyedotun, 2020; Rahiem, 2021) indicates that despite the overwhelming constraints, language educators have stepped out of their comfort zones and remained dedicated to supporting students' academic goals. Moreover, the new methods and techniques that emerged from the Covid era educational experiences have continued to be relevant and proven beneficial for EFL instruction even after the end of the pandemic.

Before the global health crisis generated by COVID-19, EFL pedagogy was predominantly anchored in traditional classroom dynamics, emphasizing face-to-face interactions, physical materials, and established assessment methods. However, the post-COVID era has ushered in a new paradigm, necessitating educators to integrate technology, embrace blended learning models, and prioritize learner autonomy. This shift has not only redefined the modalities of EFL instruction but also the very essence of how language education is perceived and delivered in the 21st century.

In the pre-Covid period, traditional EFL instruction primarily took place in classrooms, where face-to-face interaction and printed materials dominated. In the aftermath of the pandemic, we are experiencing a ubiquitous integration of technology, through the extensive use of online platforms, apps, and digital tools to enhance learning. These tools do not just replicate physical classrooms but expand pedagogical possibilities. Against this backdrop, blended and hybrid models of learning are increasingly used and integrated in the traditional paradigms. These approaches combine in-person and online instruction, allowing for greater flexibility and catering to different learning styles. While pre-Covid teaching limitedly encouraged learner autonomy—often within structured boundaries—EFL educators now design tasks that promote self-regulated learning, mostly occurring in the online environment which requires students to take more responsibility, leading to increased autonomy (Goulão & Menedez, 2015; Junaštíková, 2023). According to Bjork et al. (2013), for a learner to become effective in the learning process they should "not only be able to assess accurately the states of their own learning, but also be able to manage their own learning and activities in response to such monitoring" (p. 422).

Traditional tests and exams were the primary means of assessment before Covid; in the post-Covid era, EFL teaching has embraced alternative assessment methods, such as e-portfolios, reflective journals, and peer assessments, especially since traditional testing is challenging to administer online. In terms of teacher professional development, focus used to be on content knowledge and teaching techniques. With the increasing rise of ICT in education, EFL practitioners seek training in digital tool utilization, online pedagogy, and managing virtual classrooms, ensuring they remain effective and adapted to the digital age (Mahatma Gandhi Institute of Education for Peace and Sustainable Development, 2019).

The journey from face-to-face interactions to exclusively online teaching, learning and evaluation and then the transition back to blended approaches that aimed at harnessing the benefits of both traditional and virtual classrooms was not an easy endeavor. The main challenges faced by EFL educators and learners in the post-pandemic era could be summed up as follows:

2.1. Technological Barriers

While the shift to online learning platforms was rapid and almost universal, not all students and educators were prepared or equipped for this transition. The digital divide, manifested in inconsistent access to devices, unreliable internet connections, and unfamiliarity with e-learning platforms, posed significant challenges. For many, what was intended to be an immersive EFL experience was hindered by technological glitches and inaccessibility.

2.2. The Erosion of Immersive Learning Environments

EFL teaching thrives on immersion and interaction. The physical classroom, with its dynamic discussions, group activities, and face-to-face interactions, is pivotal for honing language skills. The move to online spaces compromised this immersive environment, making spontaneous conversations, pronunciation exercises, and real-time feedback more challenging.

2.3. Student Engagement and Retention

In the virtual landscape, maintaining consistent student engagement became a Herculean task. The lack of a structured classroom setting, coupled with the distractions of a home environment, led to reduced participation, sporadic attendance, and, in some cases, diminished motivation to learn.

2.4. Assessment Difficulties

Traditional assessment methods in EFL, such as oral tests, group discussions, or in-person written exams, were challenged by the online mode of instruction. Ensuring the authenticity of submissions, mitigating malpractices during online tests, and holistically gauging language proficiency became more complex.

2.5. Socio-emotional Isolation

Language learning is as much a socio-emotional journey as it is cognitive. The isolation induced by prolonged online learning and the lack of peer interactions led to feelings of alienation among students. This emotional detachment sometimes translated to reduced enthusiasm for EFL learning.

2.6. Teacher Adaptability

Not all EFL instructors were adept at navigating the digital teaching landscape. Adapting to new platforms, modifying lesson plans for online delivery, and managing virtual classrooms demanded rapid up-skilling, often without ample preparatory time or resources.

Against this multi-faceted background, educators found it both complex and demanding to adapt teaching and evaluation methods and techniques. The post-pandemic challenges in the EFL sphere underscore the intricate interplay of pedagogy, technology, and human versatility. As the world navigates this new normal, it becomes imperative that EFL education address these challenges. While the road ahead might seem fraught with obstacles, it also offers an opportunity: to re-imagine, reinvent, and reinforce the foundations of EFL instruction for a more resilient future.

As instructors and learners grappled with the new realities, a series of initial pedagogical shifts began to emerge, shaping the intricate fabric of EFL instruction. Central to this evolution was the embrace of digital platforms like Zoom, Microsoft Teams, and Google Classroom (Stoian et al., 2022). These tools not only bridged the gap left by closed physical classrooms but also introduced novel ways of engagement, from video lectures to group discussions. To accommodate the diverse schedules and needs of students, asynchronous learning emerged as a preferred modality, with instructors offering pre-recorded lectures and an array of digital resources to be accessed at students' convenience. The surge of educational technology further enriched the EFL experience, with language apps, AI-driven tools, and interactive simulations making learning more dynamic and personalized.

Task-based learning became a hallmark, emphasizing real-world language applications and fostering student independence. Recognizing the challenges of direct instruction in virtual environments, as well as the benefits of such an educational approach in the long run prompted many EFL instructors to use task-based learning when designing teaching activities (Celik, 2017). Students were often assigned real-world language tasks—such as watching English films, conducting online interviews, or writing reviews—which they could undertake independently and then discuss collaboratively. This new EFL paradigm also championed learner autonomy, pushing students to set personal language milestones, employ self-assessment techniques, and curate their learning resources.

The online learning experiences also drove a re-evaluation of the traditional testing methods (Tartavulea et al., 2020; Thathsarani et al., 2023). Many instructors shifted towards continuous assessment, portfolio submissions, and open-book exams. Oral examinations took the form of online interviews or presentations, and emphasis was placed on understanding over rote memorization.

Amidst these changes, the emotional dimension of learning was not sidelined. Recognizing the isolation inherent to remote learning, educators instilled a spirit of community through virtual meetings, forums, and group projects. Furthermore, as the world grappled with the mental strain of the pandemic, EFL classes became spaces for emotional reflection, underlining the importance of mental well-being alongside linguistic proficiency.

The initial pedagogical shifts in EFL teaching post-pandemic epitomize the resilience and adaptability inherent in the educational community. While these changes were born out of necessity, many have potential long-term implications, hinting at a more flexible, technologically integrated, and student-centric future for EFL instruction. As the world continues to evolve in the aftermath of global crises, so too will the methodologies by which we teach and learn languages, ensuring that communication remains a bridge, even in the most challenging of times.

Another significant shift induced by the teaching during the pandemic was the transition from a predominantly teacher-centered approach to a more student-centered paradigm (Sidi et al., 2023). In a student-centered model, the recognition that each learner possesses a unique set of strengths, weaknesses, and pacing preferences became paramount. This paradigm allows for differentiation, where learning experiences can be tailored to individual needs, thereby providing a more personalized EFL experience. Modern e-learning tools offered the means to facilitate this shift. Platforms equipped with adaptive learning algorithms, like language learning apps and online practice modules, offer content aligned with a student's proficiency and progression. This ensured that learners received instruction and practice at just the right level of challenge. Furthermore, a student-centered approach naturally emphasizes active learning. Instead of being passive recipients of information, students in this paradigm are encouraged to be inquisitive, participate in discussions, collaborate on projects, and actively engage with the material, thereby enhancing language retention and application. By placing students at the center of their education, they are not just learning English but also cultivating essential skills like critical thinking, self-assessment, and self-directed learning. These skills are invaluable in an ever-evolving global landscape, ensuring learners are equipped for continuous personal and professional development.

Championing self-directed language learning in the post-pandemic era brings about a series of benefits to be exploited in EFL instruction. Against a background of swift challenges and reconfigurations, the post-Covid world has underlined the importance of adaptability in all spheres, especially in education. One of the most significant pedagogical shifts observed is the rise of self-directed language learning. Rooted in the principle of students taking charge of their own learning journey, self-directed language learning has come to the forefront, offering a plethora of benefits that are particularly resonant in this new age (Moradi, 2018).

Firstly, self-directed learning offers unparalleled flexibility. As the world grapples with staggered lockdowns and unpredictable schedules, traditional classroom settings can be restrictive. In contrast, the self-directed learning approach promoted by a blended learning context allows students to tailor their self-study schedules, pacing, and needs based on their personal circumstances and preferences. As every learner is unique, bringing in varied levels of proficiency, learning styles, and goals, personalization is also an important dimension fostered by self-directed learning. A self-directed approach empowers students to curate resources, choose methodologies, and set milestones that align closely with their individual needs (Tan & Koh, 2015). As learners can dive deep into areas of interest or spend more time on challenging aspects, they often achieve more profound comprehension and retention.

The post-pandemic world, more than ever, values resilience and autonomy. Self-directed language learning fosters these traits, pushing learners to take initiative, seek out resources, and solve problems independently. This not only enhances linguistic proficiency but also cultivates life skills that are crucial in navigating the uncertainties of the contemporary world. Furthermore, this mode of learning capitalizes on the abundance of digital resources available. From language apps, podcasts, and online courses to global forums and social media groups, learners have a vast reservoir at their fingertips. This rich ecosystem not only provides diverse learning materials but also facilitates authentic interactions with native speakers and fellow learners from around the world.

By and large, the post-pandemic era, with all its intricacies, has accentuated the significance of self-directed language learning. By offering flexibility, personalization, and fostering invaluable life skills, it not only meets the immediate challenges of the times but also prepares learners for a world where lifelong learning and adaptability are paramount.

A pivotal area that also witnessed substantial change is the domain of evaluation and assessment in EFL. The post-pandemic EFL classroom, characterized by its digital nature, requires an innovative approach to evaluation and assessment.

Traditional pen-and-paper tests, while still valuable, need to be complemented with diverse online tools and methodologies that reflect the multifaceted nature of language learning in the digital age (Stannard & Basiel, 2013; Zainuddin, 2023; Zhou & Wei, 2018). As EFL educators navigate this new terrain, a blend of traditional and contemporary assessment strategies will be pivotal in ensuring a comprehensive, fair, and insightful evaluation of language proficiency.

With the hasty transition to online teaching, traditional assessment methodologies often proved unsuitable, necessitating a re-think of how language proficiency is gauged in the digital space. The online environment provides ample opportunities for continuous feedback. Instead of relying solely on end-of-term exams, there is a discernible shift towards formative assessment where students receive ongoing feedback through tools like Google Classroom, Microsoft Teams, or Moodle (Ramírez-Romero et al., 2018). Integrating this approach in the post-pandemic English classroom not only determines language proficiency but also provides actionable insights to learners, fostering iterative learning. Tools like Quizlet, Kahoot!, and Socrative have gained prominence, offering diverse question formats from multiple-choice to short-answer. These platforms facilitate real-time assessment, allowing EFL educators to swiftly identify and address knowledge gaps, while adding the fun and competitive component to language instruction (Choi & Chung, 2021). E-learning tools also allow assessment in digital formats. Digital portfolios, for example, where students collate their written essays, audio recordings, and video presentations, offer a holistic view of their linguistic journey. Such evaluations tools enable EFL educators to assess not just the end result but the learning process, underscoring critical thinking, creativity, and linguistic evolution.

Using online platforms even during face-to face interactions offers the advantage of not only adaptive learning, but also adaptive testing, by adjusting the input's difficulty level based on each student's performance. This ensures that the assessment is tailored to the individual, providing a more nuanced understanding of their language proficiency.

Another traditional issue that English language instruction has been confronted with in terms of evaluation is language authenticity. By continuing to use digitalized tools for testing, the authentic dimension of language is ensured through virtual simulations, role-playing, and real-world problem-solving tasks. Since evaluation becomes grounded in real-life scenarios, the students' ability to apply linguistic knowledge is measured in practical, veritable situations.

However, online assessment encompasses some challenges that need to be addressed while embarking on the journey from the new normal to the next level. Issues like tech glitches, potential for academic dishonesty, and the lack of a controlled environment necessitate the development of rigorous assessment protocols and tools with robust anti-cheating measures (Guangul et al., 2020). In addition to re-adapting evaluation methods and tools, the post-Covid EFL environment also requires reconsideration of assessment methodologies. Traditional metrics of evaluation, once considered sacrosanct, now seem outmoded in the face of the evolving educational paradigms.

The digital transition has emphasized the value of process-oriented learning over mere content acquisition. With vast resources available online, the true challenge for EFL learners is no longer memorizing vocabulary or grammatical structures but effectively integrating and using them in real-life contexts. Consequently, assessments must shift from rote memorization tests to tasks that measure a student's ability to apply, analyze, and synthesize linguistic knowledge.

Another pertinent factor is the holistic development of language skills. The online ecosystem has expanded the avenues for students to listen, speak, read, and write in English. Assessments should mirror this diversity, encompassing varied tasks like online presentations, collaborative projects, and multimedia assignments. Such a versatile approach not only gives a more accurate picture of a student's proficiency but also aligns better with real-world language use.

Furthermore, the emotional and psychological challenges brought forth by the pandemic underscore the need to ensure that assessments are inclusive and empathetic. Rigid timed tests can exacerbate stress and anxiety in an already tumultuous period. A more flexible, compassionate approach, allowing students to showcase their strengths and receive constructive feedback, becomes essential (Tobia & Campbell, 2023).

Lastly, technology presents both challenges and opportunities. While educators must be vigilant about potential malpractices in online assessments, there is a vast potential in leveraging technology for innovative assessment methods. AI-driven feedback tools, digital peer reviews, and interactive simulations can offer more engaging and authentic means of evaluation (Almusaed et al., 2023).

In a nutshell, as the post-pandemic EFL classroom continues to evolve, clinging to dated assessment methodologies is not just anachronistic but detrimental at the same time. A shift towards more flexible, comprehensive, and empathetic modes of evaluation is both desirable and essential. As educators, the onus is on us to ensure that assessments, like all other facets of education, are in sync with the demands and sensibilities of our times.

3. Content and Linguistic Shifts: Rethinking the "What" of EFL Instruction in the Post-COVID Age

While much has been discussed regarding the "how" of EFL teaching in the post-Covid period—methodologies, tools, and platforms undergoing transformation—an equally significant, yet less explored realm is the "what"—the very content and linguistic nuances that go in the make up of EFL curricula. In the post-COVID age, these facets have been recalibrated to address the changing global context and learners' needs. In the ever-evolving realm of EFL instruction, the COVID-19 pandemic has acted as an unexpected catalyst, prompting a radical re-evaluation of both pedagogical content and linguistic approaches. Traditionally, EFL curricula were designed with a fixed set of linguistic goals and content priorities. However, the post-COVID age has underscored the need for fluidity, adaptability, and relevance in what we teach and how we convey it. The next section of this chapter delves into this transformative period, exploring the nuanced shifts in content selection, linguistic emphasis, and the broader implications these changes hold for future EFL instruction.

"The language that is used in language classrooms is often considered to be simultaneously the object of study and the vehicle through which language learning emerges" (O'Boyle & Samanhudi, 2023, p. 195). In order to continue to foster meaningful exchanges, teaching had to quickly adapt to the challenges and constraints of the pandemic, which ushered in several lasting transformations in terms of both content and language functions.

Content has experienced an evolution from static to dynamic. Traditional EFL content often focused on standard topics like travel, family, and daily routines, with set vocabulary lists and prescribed grammatical structures. After the Covid pandemic, there has been a shift towards more pertinent and contextually relevant themes such as global health, online communication, and digital literacy. This not only makes learning more relevant but also equips learners with vocabulary and contexts they encounter in their new daily realities. Furthermore, before the Covid, EFL instruction often emphasized formal, academic English, with a strong focus on grammatical accuracy. Nowadays, while grammar remains crucial, there is a growing emphasis on communicative competence (Earl, 2021). With the rise of virtual meetings and social media interactions, colloquial language and understanding context have become paramount. The shared experience of a global pandemic underscored interconnectedness. Consequently, present EFL materials enthusiastically incorporate diverse perspectives, fostering cultural sensitivity and global awareness (Achieng, 2023). The lexical focus changed from treating tech jargon and digital vocabulary as specialized topics to incorporate vocabulary related to remote work, online education, and digital communication, thus offering EFL learners the required proficiency in technological terminology. With online platforms becoming increasingly prevalent, there was a need to understand and effectively use technical vocabulary related to digital tools, software, and online communication. Last but not least, given the psychological impact of the pandemic, topics like mental health, resilience, and community support have found their way into EFL content, promoting language learning intertwined with socio-emotional well-being.

In the context of the increased use of online tools for education, one aspect that has been given particular emphasis has been the teaching of digital literacy skills. This meant EFL teachers incorporated content that not only covered traditional language skills but also skills necessary for navigating the digital world. The content of many EFL courses expanded to include the understanding of digital cultures, netiquette, and global digital communication norms. As teachers and institutions began to leverage both physical and digital resources, the content also diversified to include multimedia materials like videos, podcasts, online articles, and interactive exercises (Abdulrahaman et al., 2020).

Language is inherently social. It does not encapsulate only grammar and vocabulary; it has a critical role in conveying ideas, sharing emotions, and building relationships. For EFL learners, practicing conversational skills, group discussions, and other social interactions are pivotal for fluency and functional language use. Many pedagogical approaches in EFL, such as communicative language teaching or task-based learning, rely heavily on student interactions. Through working together, students can negotiate meaning, clarify doubts, and learn from each other. Furthermore, social interactions allow EFL students to build confidence. The more they practice and receive feedback in a supportive environment, the more comfortable they become in using the language.

One of the most significant challenges of the COVID-19 online EFL teaching was the potential for isolation. Without physical classrooms, students lost the casual interactions—before, after, and during breaks in class—that enriched their learning experience. However, although such a limitation could be initially perceived as a disadvantage, it was easily transformed into an opportunity with innovative dimensions. The online format has rich potential for global interactions. Consequently, EFL students can now use the virtual space to collaborate with peers from around the world, offering a richer cultural exchange and a wider exposure to different English accents and dialects. Learning using online platforms can allow for more varied interaction times, not limited to scheduled class hours. Discussion forums, chat groups, and asynchronous collaborative projects provided opportunities for extended interactions.

Very importantly, one artefact of the pandemic-induced shift from traditional teaching to online interaction is the blended learning model, which successfully merges the benefits of online and in-person interactions (Burns, 2023; Siripipatthanakul et al., 2023). The use of this instructional model can offer the flexibility of digital tools while preserving the invaluable face-to-face social interactions essential for language learning. English language teaching benefited greatly from online educational tools and methods, as educators have continued to use them even after the end of the Covid restrictions, seeking innovative ways of integrating virtual platforms for social language exchanges. Tools like Zoom, Microsoft Teams, and Google Meet were integrated into the curriculum. Breakout rooms, in particular, simulated small group interactions or pair work often seen in physical classrooms. Websites and learning management systems like Moodle or Edmodo facilitated forums where students could post, comment, and interact on given topics, allowing for continuous asynchronous dialog. Platforms like Flipgrid enabled students to record and share short videos, giving others the chance to respond, fostering asynchronous yet interactive communication. Platforms like Kahoot!, Quizlet Live, and Gimkit brought competitive, game-like elements to language practice, encouraging spontaneous and reactive use of the language. EFL teachers set up private groups or pages on platforms like Facebook, Instagram, or Twitter, turning them into interactive spaces for sharing content, starting discussions, and even hosting live chat sessions.

Promoting authentic, meaningful conversations in remote settings has proven to be a major challenge for English language teachers (Tao & Gao, 2022). The constraints of online learning have pushed educators to develop innovative strategies to replicate the authentic interactions usually found in face-to-face settings. Some of the most effective strategies that emerged from the pandemic experience and that can be effectively used with a beneficial impact on post-Covid English language teaching are:

1. Task-Based Learning (TBL), which pivots on creating real-world tasks, by designing activities that require students to use language in realistic contexts, such as planning a trip, role-playing a job interview, or organizing a virtual event. Such tasks promote genuine language use and offer meaningful communication opportunities.
2. Use of authentic materials to promote discussions on current events, by integrating recent news articles, blogs, or videos into lessons and encourage

students to share their opinions, thereby fostering significant and pertinent exchanges.
3. Designing virtual cultural exchange programs, which relies on connecting students from different classes, countries, or regions. Such exchanges not only promote authentic conversations but also enrich cultural awareness and understanding.
4. Using interactive digital tools, such as collaborative platforms (Padlet or Jamboard) for brainstorming sessions, debates, or collaborative writing exercises.
5. Use of real-life simulation activities, for example taking virtual field trips with the help of platforms such as Google Earth or going on virtual museum tours as the basis for exploratory lessons. For better development of communicative skills, these activities could be followed up with group discussions or Q&A sessions.

In the post-COVID EFL classroom, where adaptability and innovation are paramount, such teaching strategies provide a dynamic and enriching learning experience.

Against this background, the Covid era underscored the centrality of social interactions in EFL education. The need to adapt teaching and learning to the pandemic-imposed remote EFL teaching spurred educators to think outside the box, tapping into technology and pedagogical creativity to foster authentic, meaningful interactions (Astutik et al., 2023). By and large, these adaptations reflect the evolving needs and priorities of the post-COVID EFL community. While some of these transformations may be perceived as temporary responses to the pandemic scenario, many will likely remain integral, reflecting the increasingly digital and interconnected world of language learning. The challenges faced during the pandemic led to innovations and adaptations that acknowledged and addressed the importance of the social dimension in language learning. Currently, we are benefiting from these changes as their long-term implications are constantly shaping the future landscape of EFL teaching and learning.

The post-COVID era has not just transformed the methodological landscape of EFL; it has redefined its very essence. Rethinking the "what" of EFL instruction is more than a reaction to a global event; it is an acknowledgment of a rapidly changing world. The curricular shifts in content and linguistic priorities reflect a pedagogical evolution, one that recognizes the multifaceted, dynamic nature of language learning in the contemporary age.

4. Beyond Traditional Boundaries: Reimagining the Roles and Responsibilities of Educators and Learners in the Post-Covid EFL Classroom

The COVID-19 pandemic prompted a seismic shift in global education, compelling teachers and students to adapt to unprecedented challenges. For the EFL domain, this period of flux translated into a transformation in pedagogical methodologies, tools, and, most notably, roles and responsibilities. The traditional classroom dynamics, where teachers were the primary dispensers of knowledge and students passive recipients, have been upended, paving the way for a more interactive, fluid, and equitable learning ecosystem. In the post-Covid EFL classroom, both educators and learners are experiencing redefined roles, anchored in mutual respect, collaboration, and continuous learning (Munday, 2022; Neuwirth et al., 2020). The evolving dynamics of the roles and responsibilities of teachers and students in the post-Covid EFL classroom are largely attributed to the shift to online or blended learning, coupled with the evolving dynamics of 21st-century education.

First and foremost, the role of teachers has undergone a significant transformation. No longer solely dispensers of linguistic knowledge, EFL educators have evolved into digital navigators, adeptly employing online platforms and tools to deliver content. They have transitioned from traditional teaching to being facilitators of learning, guiding students through a plethora of online resources and fostering greater student autonomy.

One of the most radical makeovers of this new dimension is the conceptualization of the teacher not just as an instructor, but as a co-learner alongside students. In the post-Covid EFL classroom, the rapid integration of technology and digital platforms meant that many teachers, just like their students, found themselves navigating new tools, resources, and methodologies. This shared experience of discovery and adaptation fostered an environment where teachers, too, were learning—not just about technology, but about novel pedagogical approaches, digital resources, and even about their students' unique challenges in the new normal. Recognizing themselves as co-learners, teachers became more open to feedback, more agile in their methods, and more collaborative in their approach.

Beyond academics, the educators' task has expanded to encompass that of well-being advocates, ensuring that the socio-emotional challenges students face in these times are addressed. This transformed role emphasizes adaptability, continuous learning, and a heightened sensitivity to students' diverse needs in the ever-evolving EFL educational landscape.

The role of students in the post-Covid EFL classrooms has also witnessed a paradigm shift. They have been thrust into a more active and autonomous role in their learning journey. The digital landscape has transformed them into proactive seekers of knowledge, navigating various online platforms, apps, and resources to supplement their studies (OECD, 2016). Collaborative learning has gained prominence, with students often working in virtual groups, exchanging ideas, and co-creating projects. Furthermore, the emphasis on self-paced learning has heightened their responsibility for self-assessment and reflection. This newfound agency in their educational process underscores the evolution of EFL students from mere learners to active participants in a digitally interconnected world.

One essential consequence of the Covid-generated paradigm shift was empowering students to assume teaching roles. Fostering a deeper sense of ownership and engagement in their learning journey has been extended post-Covid, as modern educational approaches require students to step into the shoes of educators, in order to consolidate their understanding of a topic and to develop essential skills such as communication, leadership, and empathy (Joshi, 2023). This pedagogical approach, often referred to as "peer teaching" or "reverse teaching", encourages learners to present concepts, answer queries, and even design lesson plans, facilitating a more collaborative and interactive classroom environment. Such empowerment not only democratizes the learning space but also strengthens the community of learners, as students gain appreciation for the challenges and rewards of teaching and become more invested in the collective success of their peers.

In the post-Covid EFL classroom, this paradigm is reinforced and expanded by increasingly involving students in:

1. Peer teaching: One of the best ways to ensure understanding of a concept is to teach it. By allowing students to take on teaching roles, they revisit and consolidate their knowledge, improving their linguistic competencies. Moreover, fellow students bring unique cultural and personal perspectives to lessons, enriching discussions and broadening worldviews.
2. Collaborative digital projects: As digital tools became more integral in the post-COVID classroom, students are encouraged to collaborate on online projects, sometimes guiding their peers on how to use specific platforms or applications.
3. Student-led discussions: Leading a group discussion enhances students' confidence in their language skills, especially when coordinating and discussing topics they are passionate about.

4. Students as content creators: Students could be tasked with producing content (e.g., videos, blogs, podcasts) in English, which could then be used as teaching material, offering peers a relatable source of authentic language input. Also, they could be responsible for creating and leading role-play sessions or simulations, allowing them to practice both their language and teaching skills.
5. Reflection and feedback: Before exams or after completing units, students could lead review sessions, summarizing key points and facilitating Q&A interactions. Encouraging student-teachers to seek feedback on their "teaching" is instrumental in refining their approach, benefitting both their pedagogical and linguistic skills.

Empowering students to assume teaching roles not only enhances their linguistic abilities but also fosters the development of a wide range of supplementary skills and learning styles. Dede (2005, p. 10) defines such learning styles as "active learning based on experience", "learning based on collectively seeking, sieving, and synthesizing experiences", "co-design of learning experiences personalized to individual needs and preferences", "expression through non-linear, associational webs of representations rather than linear stories", and "fluency in multiple media".

In essence, the post-Covid EFL classroom heralds a significant departure from traditional teaching and learning paradigms. It recognizes the value each party brings to the table, blurring the rigid lines that once defined roles and responsibilities. As both teachers and students don the hats of learners, collaborators, and innovators, the EFL classroom becomes a vibrant, dynamic space, reflecting the needs, challenges, and endless possibilities of a post-pandemic world.

5. Conclusion

5.1. The Journey towards the "Next Normal": What Lies Ahead

Essentially, the journey from the "new normal" to the "next normal" in EFL teaching has been one of resilience, innovation, and collective growth. While the initial stages were marked by rapid adjustments and short-term solutions, the "next normal" represents a thoughtful, strategic approach to EFL teaching, marrying tradition with innovation. As we traverse this era, the "next normal" not only addresses the immediate post-COVID reality but also lays a robust foundation for the future of EFL education, primed to face any forthcoming challenges with agility and foresight.

In the wake of the COVID-19 pandemic, the educational landscape witnessed a sudden metamorphosis, often termed the "new normal". This immediate response to the crisis was characterized by a swift shift to digital platforms as physical classrooms became untenable. This rapid digital transition, however necessary, brought with it a myriad of challenges. Technical issues frequently disrupted lessons, a significant portion of both educators and students grappled with digital literacy, and the rich dynamics of face-to-face classrooms proved difficult to replicate online. To combat these challenges, institutions and teachers worked tirelessly, mobilizing a vast array of online resources, reshaping lesson plans to fit the virtual mold, and familiarizing themselves with new teaching tools. Above all, the driving force during this phase was crisis management, with a paramount emphasis on ensuring the continuity of education, even if the conditions were far from ideal.

As the dust settled on the immediate aftermath of the pandemic, the world of education began its evolution towards what many now term the "next normal", marked by refinement and groundbreaking innovation. Institutions, having taken stock of their initial digital forays, began to embrace hybrid learning models, artfully merging the strengths of both online and offline instruction. Concurrently, there was a palpable shift in pedagogy; traditional teacher-centered methods gave way to more interactive, student-centric strategies. This digital landscape not only allowed for greater student autonomy but also empowered learners to take the reins, with some even stepping into instructive roles themselves. Significantly, the limitations of physical geography faded, as the EFL community saw a surge in global collaborations, fostering invaluable cross-cultural exchanges and pooling resources. Amidst these academic strides, a conscious focus emerged on holistic well-being, addressing the mental and emotional challenges amplified by isolated, remote learning. Furthermore, the landscape of assessment underwent a transformative revision. Gone were the days of solely traditional exams; in their place arose a spectrum of evaluations that were diverse, inclusive, and seamlessly integrated with technology.

As education continues to mitigate the repercussions of the pandemic, there emerges a distinct vision for the future, firmly rooted in embracing the "next normal". At the forefront of this vision is the resolute commitment to future-proofing education. The transitory nature of the initial digital adaptation has solidified into a lasting integration, with sustained efforts directed towards enhancing technological infrastructure and providing requisite training. The upheavals brought about by the pandemic have underscored the indispensable nature of adaptability, promoting a renewed emphasis on life-long learning. Both educators and students are now acutely aware of the need for continuous skill and knowledge acquisition to deftly handle any subsequent challenges. Furthermore, there is a burgeoning recognition of the might of collective endeavor. Global EFL communities are not just being built but nurtured, placing collaboration and the sharing of best practices at their core. And as the journey continues, one of the most promising developments is the rise of diverse learning pathways. With technology as a powerful ally, the future EFL classroom will be marked by personalized learning experiences, meticulously tailored to accommodate each student's unique needs, preferences, and learning rhythms, prefiguring an era of truly inclusive education.

In the evolving landscape of post-COVID EFL education, numerous transformative changes are poised to reshape the teaching and learning experience. Foremost, technology integration is set to burgeon, with Artificial Intelligence steering adaptive learning experiences and offering immersive linguistic adventures like never before. The globalization of classrooms will set the foundation for a new era of cross-cultural exchange, facilitated by collaborative online platforms and enriched by insights from international experts. As the content expands, there will be a pronounced emphasis on soft skills, integrating holistic language learning with socio-emotional modules to address the unique challenges of the digital age.

Future EFL classrooms will also prize flexibility. Hybrid teaching models will become the norm, allowing students the autonomy to select their learning mode. Such flexibility will be mirrored in self-paced modules, granting students the agency to learn at their rhythm. This student-centric approach will manifest in curricula that are largely driven by learners, characterized by increased autonomy in content selection and a lean towards project-based learning.

Ensuring inclusivity, EFL pedagogies will cater to a plethora of diverse learning needs. Digital tools will democratize access, ensuring that all students, regardless of their challenges, partake in quality education. Such inclusivity will be complemented by curricula designed with heightened cultural sensitivity, celebrating the myriad backgrounds of EFL learners.

For educators, continuous professional development will be paramount. Not only will they need to keep abreast of the latest digital tools, but their role will also transition to that of facilitators in this ever-evolving digital milieu. The renaissance in teaching will be matched by an assessment overhaul, with a shift from traditional tests to diverse, holistic evaluations. Digital platforms will allow instantaneous feedback, promoting real-time rectifications.

The journey towards the "new normal" in EFL teaching promises a more inclusive, flexible, and student-cantered paradigm. As the future becomes present, the ultimate goal remains constant: to offer a holistic, comprehensive, and engaging language learning experience that prepares students for a diverse, globalized, and interconnected world.

References

Abdulrahaman, M. D., Faruk, N., Oloyede, A. A., Surajudeen-Bakinde, N. T., Olawoyin, L. A., Mejabi, O. V., Imam-Fulani, Y. O., Fahm, A. O., & Azeez, A. L. (2020). Multimedia tools in the teaching and learning processes: A systematic review. *Heliyon*, 6(11), 1–14.

Achieng, S. A. (2023). Exploring effective teaching approaches for English as a Foreign Language (EFL) instructors: Best practices and future directions. *International Journal on Studies in Education* (*IJonSE*), 5(4), 515–529.

Almusaed, A., Almssad, A., Yitmen, I., & Homod, R. Z. (2023). Enhancing student engagement: Harnessing "AIED"'s power in hybrid education—a review analysis. *Education Sciences*, 13(7), 632.

Astutik, Y., Wahyuni, A., Mastuti, E. R., Mandarani, V., & Jalilovna, J. L. (2023, April). COVID-19 and EFL teaching: Adapting technological and pedagogical competencies in Indonesia. In H. Ku, B. Sobirov, D. Sugandini, & M. T. Multazam (Eds.), ICARSE 2022. *Proceedings of the international conference on advance research in social and economic science series: Advances in social science, education and humanities research* (pp. 346–357, 748). Paris: Atlantis Press.

Bjork, R. A., Dunlosky, J., & Kornell, N. (2013). Self-regulated learning: Beliefs, techniques and illusions. *Annual Review of Psychology*, 64, 417–444.

Burns, M. (2023). *Distance education for teacher training: Modes, models and methods* (2nd ed.). Washington, DC: Education Development Center.

Celik, B. (2017). Task-based learning: An effective way of developing communication skills. *International Journal of Social Sciences and Educational Studies*, 4(2), 109–114.

Choi, L., & Chung, S. (2021). Navigating online language teaching in uncertain times: Challenges and strategies of EFL educators in creating a sustainable technology-mediated language learning environment. *Sustainability*, 13(14), 7664.

Dede, C. (2005). Planning for neomillennial learning styles. *Educause Quarterly*, 28(1), 7–12.

Earl, J. (2021). Language teaching after Covid-19: Real world priorities. *Expert comment*, accessed December 17, 2023, https://blogs.canterbury.ac.uk/expert comment/language-teaching-after-covid-19-real-world-priorities/

Gags, A., Goertler, S., & Spasova, S. (2020). Planned online language education versus crisis-prompted online language teaching: Lessons for the future. *Foreign Language Annals*, 53(2), 380–392.

Goulão, M. de F., & Menedez, R. C. (2015). Learner autonomy and self-regulation in eLearning. *Procedia—Social and Behavioral Sciences*, 174, 1900–1907.

Guangul, F. M., Suhail, A. H., Khalit, M. I., & Khidhir, B. A. (2020). Challenges of remote assessment in higher education in the context of COVID-19: A case study of Middle East College. *Educational Assessment, Evaluation and Accountability*, 32(4), 519–535.

Joshi, S. (2023). The role of technology in education, post pandemic. *eLearning Industry*, June 22, 2023, accessed November 4, 2023, https://elearningindustry.com/the-role-of-technology-in-education-post-pandemic

Junaštíková, J. (2023). Self-regulation of learning in the context of modern technology: A review of empirical studies. *Interactive Technology and Smart Education*, ahead-of-print(ahead-of-print), accessed November 15, 2023, https://www.emerald.com/insight/content/doi/10.1108/ITSE-02-2023-0030/full/html

Mahatma Gandhi Institute of Education for Peace and Sustainable Development. (2019). *Rethinking pedagogy: Exploring the potential of digital technology in achieving quality education*. New Delhi: UNESCO MGIEP.

Mavridi, S. (2022). *Language teaching experiences during COVID-19*. London: British Council.

Mavridi, S. (2023). Language education during the pandemic: Lessons learned and directions for change. In S. Kourieos & D. Evripidou (Eds.), *Language teaching and learning during the COVID-19 pandemic: A shift to a new era* (pp. 1–17). Newcastle upon Tyne: Cambridge Scholars Publishing.

Moradi, H. (2018). Self-directed learning in language teaching-learning processes. *Modern Journal of Language Teaching Methods*, 8(6), 59–64.

Moser, K. M., Wei, M., Wei, T., & Brenner, D. (2021). Remote teaching during COVID-19: Implications from a national survey of language educators. *System*, 97, 1–15.

Munday, D. (2022). Hybrid pedagogy and learning design influences in a higher education context. *Studies in Technology Enhanced Learning*, 2(2), 243–258.

Neuwirth, L., Jović, S., & Mukherji-Ratnam, R. (2020). Reimagining higher education during and post-COVID-19: Challenges and opportunities. *Journal of Adult and Continuing Education*, 27, 1–16.

Niculescu, B. O., & Dragomir, I. A. (2021, June). One head, multiple hats—Lessons learned from online teaching. In *KBO 2023. Proceedings of the 27th international conference knowledge-based organization* (pp. 165–170), 27(2). Sibiu: "Nicolae Bălcescu" Land Forces Academy Publishing House.

O'Boyle, A., & Samanhudi, U. (2023). Adapting and transforming ELT during and post Covid-19 era: People, places, and purposes. *TEFLIN Journal*, 34(1), 194–208.

OECD. (2016). *Innovating education and educating for innovation: The power of digital technologies and skills*. Paris: OECD Publishing.

Oyedotun, T. D. (2020). Sudden change of pedagogy in education driven by COVID-19: Perspectives and evaluation from a developing country. *Research in Globalization*, 2, 1–5.

Rahiem, M. D. H. (2021). Remaining motivated despite the limitations: University students' learning propensity during the COVID-19 pandemic. *Children and Youth Services Review*, 120, 1–14.

Ramírez-Romero, J. L., Rodríguez-Rosales, M., & Salazar-Sorcia, H. (2018). The role of ICT in the evaluation and assessment of English as foreign or as a second language. In S. T. Soto, E. Intriago Palacios, & J. Villafuerte Holguín (coords.), *Beyond paper-and-pencil tests: Good assessment practices for EFL classes* (pp. 155–181). Machala: Universidad Técnica de Machala.

Richards, L. J., Dooley, K. E., & Lindner, J. R. (2004). Online course design principles. In C. Howard, K. Schenk, & R. Discenza (Eds.), *Distance learning and university effectiveness: Changing educational paradigms for online learning* (pp. 99–118). Hershey, PA: Information Science Publishing.

Sidi, Y., Shamir-Inbal, T., & Eshet-Alkalai, Y. (2023). From face-to-face to online: Teachers' perceived experiences in online distance teaching during the Covid-19 pandemic. *Computers & Education*, 201, 1–16.

Siripipatthanakul, S., Muthmainnah, M., Asrifan, A., Siripipattanakul, S., Kaewpuang, P., Sriboonruang, P., Limna, P., Jaipong, P., & Sitthipon, T. (2023). Blended learning and online learning during the COVID-19 pandemic. In A. Asrifan & N. Faradillah (Eds.), *Interdisciplinary research: Collaborative insights*, 1 (pp. 44–54). India: Island Publishers.

Stannard, R., & Basiel, A. (2013). A practice-based exploration of technology enhanced assessment for English language teaching. In G. Motteram (Ed.), *Innovations in learning technologies for English language teaching* (pp. 147–173). London: British Council, accessed December 17, 2023, https://www.teachingenglish.org.uk/sites/teacheng/files/C607%20Information%20and%20Communication_WEB%20ONLY_FINAL.pdf

Stoian, C. E., Fărcaşiu, M. A., Dragomir, G.-M., & Gherheş, V. (2022). Transition from online to face-to-face education after COVID-19: The benefits of online education from students' perspective. *Sustainability*, 14(19), 1–18.

Tan, L., & Ling, J. K. H. (2015). *Self-directed learning: Learning in the 21st century*. Singapore: Ministry of Education, accessed November 14, 2023, https://www.researchgate.net/publication/285591239_Self-Directed_Learning_Learning_in_the_21st_Century

Tao, J., & Gao, X. (2022). Teaching and learning languages online: Challenges and responses. *System*, 107(3), 1–9.

Tartavulea, C. V., Albu, C. N., Albu, N., Dieaconescu, R. I., & Petre, S. (2020). Online teaching practices and the effectiveness of the educational process in the wake of the COVID-19 pandemic. *Amfiteatru Economic*, 22(55), 920–936.

Thathsarani, H., Ariyananda, D. K., Jayakody, C., Manoharan, K., Munasinghe, A. A. S. N., & Rathnayake, N. (2023). How successful the online assessment techniques in distance learning have been, in contributing to academic achievements of management undergraduates?. *Education and Information Technologies*, 28, 14091–14115.

Tobia, A., & Campbell, A. (2023). 5 effective constructive feedback examples: Unlocking student potential. *Turnitin*, August 23, 2023, accessed December 20, 2023, https://www.turnitin.com/blog/constructive-feedback-examples-for-students

Zainuddin, N. (2023). Technology enhanced language learning research trends and practices: A systematic review (2020–2022). *The Electronic Journal of e-Learning*, 21(2), 69–79.

Zhou, Y., & Wei, M. (2018). Strategies in technology-enhanced language learning. *Studies in Second Language Learning and Teaching* (*SSLLT*), 8(2), 471–495.

Fatlume Berisha, Albane Fetiu, and Vjollca Markaj

Beliefs of First-Year Science and Mathematics Master's Students about Teaching and Learning

1. Introduction

Numerous studies around the world (Tsai, 2002; Savasci-Acikalin, 2009; Markic & Elliks, 2012; Ambusaidi & Al-Balushi, 2012; Al-Amoush, Markic, Abu-Hola, & Eilks, 2011; Bakir, 2016) have examined teachers beliefs concerning the process of teaching and learning mathematics and science subjects. Teachers play a crucial role in the classroom, which includes tasks such as lesson planning, activity design, and assisting students in achieving curriculum competencies. It is believed that teachers' beliefs regarding the effects of teaching and learning further shape their educational experience and play a crucial role in determining the nature of mathematics and science education practices for students in the classroom (Ambusaidi & Al-Balushi, 2012). As we move further into the 21st century, classroom practices are important as it is imperative that students possess problem-solving, critical thinking, and effective communication skills, requiring them to independently seek and process information beyond what their teachers teach (Bakir, 2016).

Many decades ago, Bandura (1986) emphasized the influence of beliefs on the actions, reactions, and decision-making processes of an individual. Similarly, Pajares (1992) emphasized that beliefs extend beyond the realm of science knowledge and have a significant impact on all aspects of teaching and learning, thereby influencing teacher-student interactions. These personal beliefs about teaching and learning held by teachers have a significant impact on their strategies, methods, and openness to further professional development (Markic & Eilks, 2010).Use this for the paragraph in a section. Use this for the paragraph in a section. Use this for the paragraph in a section. Use this for the paragraph in a section.

To comprehend the profound impact that beliefs have on the lives and actions of individuals, Mariani (1999) developed a four-layered pyramid model (Figure 1) that illustrates the connection between beliefs, attitudes, decisions, and actions. According to this model, beliefs shape attitudes, which in turn affect an individual's decisions and ultimately determine his or her actions. By applying this model, we gain a practical understanding of the significance of personal beliefs in influencing behavior and decision-making.

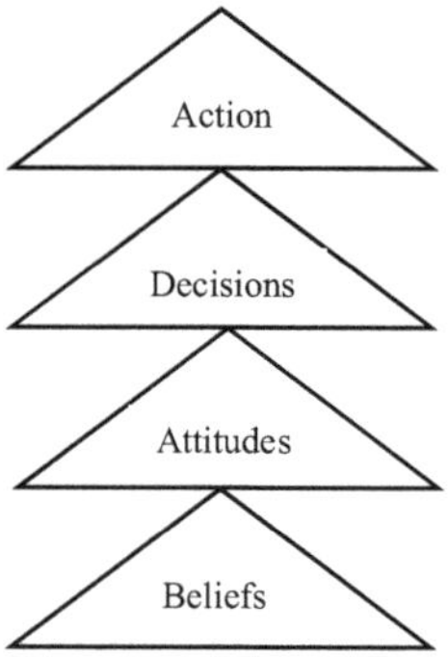

Figure 1: Relationship between beliefs, attitudes, decisions, and actions
Source: Mariani, 1999

Thomas et al. (2001) categorized pre-service teachers' mental models of teaching as explicit, conceptual, and exploratory. In the explicit teaching model, the teacher uses didactic techniques to provide information, corrective feedback, and concept demonstrations (Whyte & Ellis, 2003). The teacher plays a prominent role in front of the class, using the blackboard and encouraging students to concentrate on their textbooks and notebooks. The conceptual teaching model, on the other hand, combines didactic techniques with a constructivist approach, with an emphasis on subject matter and concepts. Activities like research, discovery, and problem-solving assist students in learning and expanding their knowledge base. In this model, the teacher assumes a guiding role by introducing the unit and providing research-related background information. Students participate in laboratory- and activity-based learning, working in small groups while the instructor closely observes and provides guidance (Whyte & Ellis, 2003). Whereas the exploratory teaching model is centered on students' interests and decisions. Here, the teacher acts as a researcher alongside the students to promote active discovery and learning (Martin, 1997). This approach emphasizes discussions, individual or group projects, and activities outside the classroom. Students collaborate in groups, with the teacher providing support and assistance (Whyte & Ellis, 2003).

Pajares (1992) pointed out that pedagogical beliefs significantly influence teachers' classroom practices and behaviors. In a study by Thomson, Turner, and Nietfeld (2012) that investigated prospective teachers enrolled in a US teacher education program, identified their teaching typologies based on their motivations and beliefs about teaching. The findings suggest that these beliefs have a lasting impact on their teaching careers and approaches. Furthermore, it was observed that most prospective teachers are driven by altruistic and intrinsic motivation and have favorable views of teaching.

Teachers' beliefs can be broadly classified into two approaches: teacher-centered and student-centered (Ambusaidi & Al-Balushi, 2012). Teacher-centered beliefs often align with behaviorism, where the teacher assumes a directive role in the classroom (Deng, Chai, Tsai, & Lee, 2014). In contrast, teachers with student-centered beliefs prioritize students' needs and interests (Mayer, 2003), reflecting the principles of constructivism (Deng, Chai, Tsai, & Lee, 2014). In the traditional teacher centered approach, students play a passive role and receive knowledge primarily from the teacher, who focuses on content delivery. Modern teacher beliefs, in contrast, emphasize active student participation, independent work, and meaningful topics (Al-Amoush, Markic, Abu-Hola, & Eilks, 2011). Modern approaches encourage teachers to not only provide information but also foster learning by permitting students to express their opinions and participate in decision-making processes.

Numerous studies have explored beliefs about teaching and learning using the DASTT-C instrument (Tsai, 2002; Al-Amoush, Markic, Abu-Hola, & Eilks, 2011; Porlán & Del Pozo, 2004; Boz & Uzuntiryaki, 2006). Among science teachers, traditional teacher-centered beliefs have been frequently observed (Tsai, 2002; El Takach, 2018). For instance, Markic and Eilks (2013) used drawings to understand German pre-service teachers' beliefs and found a prevalence of traditional, teacher-centered beliefs. In a different investigation, Bakir (2016) employed interviews and observations along with the DASTT-C instrument, discovering that five out of six pre-service science teachers held a conceptual approach while one embraced an exploratory approach.

Moreover, Markic and Eilks (2010) reported that chemistry and physics teachers exhibited more teacher-centered beliefs compared to biology teachers, who predominantly endorsed student-centered beliefs. In contrary, Akkus (2013) found that pre-service chemistry teachers demonstrated stronger student-centered beliefs than their counterparts in biology and physics. A cross-cultural study by Al-Amoush et al. (2011) comparing pre-service chemistry teachers from Jordan, Turkey, and Germany revealed that Jordanian teachers held more traditional beliefs, while German teachers adopted modern, student-centered beliefs.

Bryan (1999) asserted that prospective teachers' beliefs about teaching and learning are often shaped during their entry into teacher preparation programs. Similar findings came from other studies, including those by Yilmaz-Tuzun (2008), Hancock and Gallard (2004), Lin et al. (2001), and Bryan and Abell

(1999). Additionally, Leonard et al. (2011) proposed that pre-service teachers may experience a transformation in their beliefs through exposure to conversion experiences. Lin et al. (2001) further argued that beliefs can be influenced and changed during teacher education programs, particularly through various training interventions, leading to a shift towards student-centered beliefs (Ambusaidi & Al-Balushi, 2012; El Takach, 2018).

Saçıcı (2013) found that most science teachers exhibit both student- and teacher-centered beliefs about teaching and learning. These findings suggest that science teachers might still be influenced by their teacher-centered experiences in elementary and middle school education. However, in contrast, Schumacher and Wilde (2021) reported that pre-service teachers often envision student-centered lessons despite experiencing predominantly teacher-centered lessons during their training. This observation implies that past schooling experiences may not necessarily dictate how prospective teachers envision their future teaching approaches.

In many educational systems worldwide, extensive research has been conducted to explore and understand the beliefs and attitudes of teachers towards teaching and learning. This research has led to significant insights and measures for enhancing educational practices and outcomes. However, the state of education in Kosovo, particularly regarding the teaching of mathematics and science subjects, lacks comprehensive research on teachers' beliefs and their impact on instructional practices. In Kosovo's education system, science subjects are segregated into distinct disciplines, such as physics, chemistry, and biology, and taught individually to students starting in the 6th and 7th grades. Conversely, mathematics is introduced in the first grade.

In 2016, Kosovo implemented a new Curriculum aimed at promoting competency-based education. The Curriculum aims to empower students to explore and comprehend the world around them, applying their learning experiences to real-life contexts. However, the realization of these competencies depends significantly on the beliefs and approaches adopted by mathematics and science teachers in the classroom. The lack of research on this topic suggests that scientific literacy in Kosovo remains underdeveloped, with students predominantly assessed based on rote memorization rather than critical thinking and practical application of scientific knowledge.

The need to understand and evaluate science teachers' beliefs in Kosovo becomes imperative to identify effective teaching approaches and improve mathematics and science education. This study seeks to fill this research gap by identifying and evaluating the beliefs of Kosovar students pursuing master's studies in teaching mathematics and sciences, the future teachers. The study aims to ascertain whether mathematics and science teachers predominantly adopt traditional or more modern teaching and learning approaches and how the beliefs of pre-service teachers vary based on their specific scientific field of teaching.

2. Methodology

2.1. Sample and Data Collection

The Draw-a-Science-Teacher Test Checklist (DASTT-C) was used to collect data (Thomas, Pedersen, & Finson, 2001). Students in their first year of subject teaching programs (mathematics, biology, chemistry, and physics) at the Faculty of Education, University of Prishtina "Hasan Prishtina" were asked to participate in the research during the fall semester of 2019. Table 1 represents gender and age demographics of the participants. The participants were asked to draw themselves as a science teacher and their students in a typical teaching situation: "How do you envision yourself as a science teacher in the relevant subject?" After analyzing ninety-five collected samples, seventeen were disregarded due to incomplete DASTT-C sheet completion.

Table 1: Demographics

	Gender		Age			
Sample Group	**Female**	**Male**	**20–25**	**26–36**	**37–47**	**48–65**
Biology	23	5	21	6	1	0
Chemistry	12	4	2	13	1	0
Physics	6	3	0	6	3	0
Mathematics	17	8	13	11	1	0
Total	58	20	36	36	6	0
%	74 %	26 %	46 %	46 %	8 %	0 %

2.2. Analyzing of Data

Thomas et al. (2001) assessment attributes were used for the analysis. Thomas et al. (2001) created a measurement scale based on a thirteen-item checklist of characteristics, with the teacher and student at its center. These characteristics are separated into three categories: teacher, student, and environment. Each of the thirteen items within the three domains is assigned a score of 1 or 0 to indicate the presence or absence of the corresponding attribute. The range of total points is from 0 to 13. In accordance with the total number of accumulated points, a decision was made regarding teaching styles (see Thomas et al., 2001). Two researchers independently analyzed the drawings of all pre-service teachers using the DASTT-C checklist. Inter-rater reliability was measured using Cohen's κ coefficient, and the results indicate that reliability was relatively high across all subgroups of the sample (Table 2). In some instances of disagreement, the two researchers examined the data and reached a consensus conclusion. The data was analyzed and presented following the work of Markic and Eliks (2010).

Table 2: Inter-rater reliability for DASTT-C scores

	Cohen's κ Value
Sample (n = 78)	0.82
Mathematics (n = 25)	0.80
Physics (n = 9)	0.75
Chemistry (n = 16)	0.76
Biology (n = 28)	0.91

3. Findings/Results

In their study, Thomas et al. (2001) developed the Draw-A-Science-Teacher-Teaching-Checklist (DASTT-C) as an assessment tool for evaluating teachers' beliefs through the analysis of their drawing scores. Table 3 presents a comprehensive overview of the drawing scores obtained from the pre-service teachers who took part in our data collection process. Through a meticulous analysis of absolute values and relative frequencies, notable patterns become evident across different subject domains. A different observation arises from the analysis of participants in mathematics education pre-service teacher programs. Based on the data presented in Table 3, around 50 % of the participants demonstrated a tendency to draw classroom scenarios where the student assumes to be in the center within the pedagogical classroom environment. Pre-service teachers who are engaged in the study of science education disciplines, such as physics, chemistry, and biology, demonstrate distinct patterns of drawings. Within this context, it can be observed that the majority of their classroom drawing scenarios are indicative of pedagogical beliefs that prioritize the role of the teacher. The observed variations in the dynamics of the subjects underscore the importance of subject-specific factors in shaping the instructional beliefs held by pre-service teachers. The quantitative analysis presented in Table 3 provides clarification on the disparities, thus enhancing our overall comprehension of the distinct pedagogical viewpoints embraced by different academic fields.

Table 3: Distribution of points showing attitudes towards the student in the center or the teacher according to the sample group

DASTT-C Score	Mathematics (n = 25)	Physics (n =9)	Chemistry (n = 16)	Biology (n = 28)
0	0 (0 %)	0(0 %)	0(0 %)	0 (0 %)
1	0 (0 %)	0 (0 %)	0(0 %)	0(0 %)
2	0 (0 %)	0(0 %)	0(0 %)	0(0 %)
3	1 (4 %)	0 (0 %)	0(0 %)	1 (3.6 %)
4	11 (44 %)	0 (0 %)	2 (12.5 %)	3(10.7 %)
Subtotal: Student in Center (0–4)	**12 (48 %)**	**0 (0 %)**	**2 (12.5 %)**	**4 (14.3 %)**
5	1 (4 %)	0 (0 %)	0(0 %)	3 (10.7 %)
6	2 (8 %)	0 (0 %)	0(0 %)	2 (7.1 %)
Subtotal: With the Student in Center (5–6)	**3 (12 %)**	**0 (0 %)**	**0(0 %)**	**5 (17.8 %)**
7	1 (4 %)	0 (0 %)	1 (6.2 %)	2 (7.1 %)
8	4 (16 %)	1 (11.1 %)	4 (25 %)	3 (10.7 %)
9	2 (8 %)	1 (11.1 %)	4 (25 %)	3 (10.7 %)
10	3 (12 %)	7 (4 %)	4 (25 %)	9 (32.1 %)
11	0 (0 %)	0 (77.8 %)	0(0 %)	1 (3.6 %)
12	0 (0 %)	0 (0 %)	1 (6.2 %)	1 (3.6 %)
13	0 (0 %)	0 (0 %)	0(0 %)	0(0 %)
Subtotal: Teacher in Center (7–13)	**10 (40 %)**	**9 (100 %)**	**14 (87.5 %)**	**19 (67.8 %)**

From Table 3, according to Thomas et al. (2001), we see that more than half of all sample groups show teacher-centered belief, while a small part shows student-centered belief, and the rest are without a decision (neither the teacher nor the student is in the center).

From the averages calculated and the t-tests performed (Tables 4 and 5), we can see that physics teachers expresses, on average, the strongest beliefs with the teacher in the center compared to the other sample groups. However, the group of chemistry and biology also showed moderately strong beliefs with the teacher in the center. The mathematics group has shown average tendencies, which, according to Thomas et al. (2001), are neither teacher-centered nor student-centered.

Table 4: Comparisons of the sample groups according to attitudes towards the student or the teacher in the center

Sample Group	Average Values	Standard Deviation
Mathematics (n = 25)	6.04	2.39
Physics (n = 9)	9.67	0.71
Chemistry (n = 16)	8.44	2.10
Biology (n = 28)	7.86	2.53

Table 5: Sample t-test results

Sample Group	Biology	Chemistry	Physics
Mathematics	0.0097	0.0017	$1.07*10^{-7}$
Physics	0.0017	0.0449	–
Chemistry	0.4190	–	–

From Table 6, we see that most of the teachers have a conceptual teaching style. Whereas, the mathematics group, approximately half of the participants have an exploratory style. In courses in the fields of chemistry and biology, approximately half of the participants had a conceptual style. In contrast, in the physics group, most of the participants performed with an explicit style.

Table 6: Sample results according to the teaching style

Teaching Style	Mathematics (n = 25)	Physics (n = 9)	Chemistry (n = 16)	Biology (n = 28)	Total (n-78)
Explicit	3 (12 %)	7 (78 %)	5 (31 %)	11 (39 %)	28 (36 %)
Conceptual	10 (40 %)	2 (22 %)	9 (56 %)	13 (47 %)	35 (45 %)
Explorer	12 (48 %)	0 (0 %)	2 (13 %)	4 (14 %)	15 (19 %)

Figure 2 presents some examples where teachers have shown explicit style, total 36 % out of n = 78 participants. The conceptual style was evident in 45 % of the total participants, some examples presented in Figure 3. Whereas exploratory style present in 19 % of all participants, mostly from mathematics group, examples of which are presented in Figure 4.

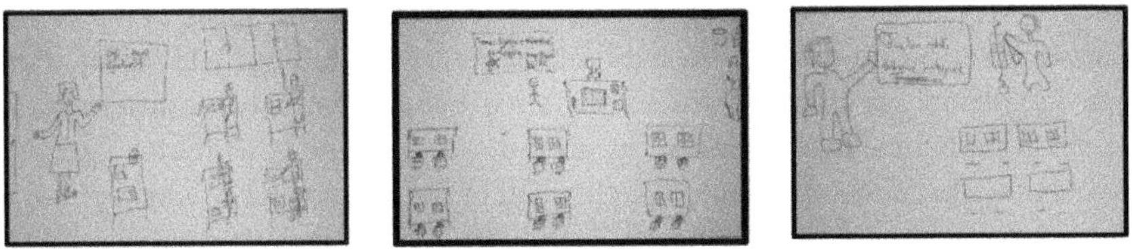

Figure 2: Examples where teachers have shown explicit style

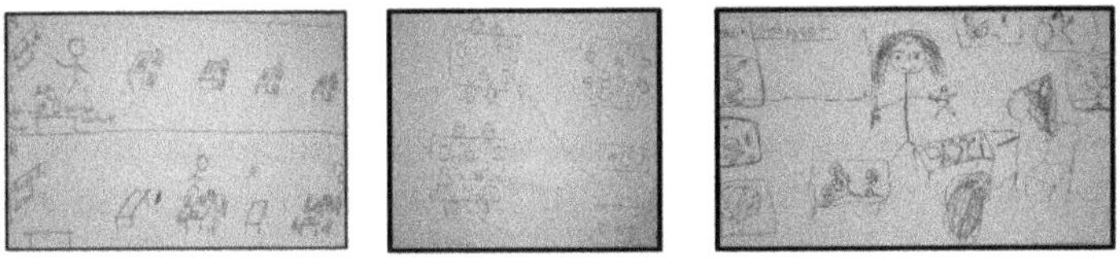

Figure 3: Examples where teachers have shown conceptual style

Figure 4: Examples where teachers have shown exploratory style

4. Discussion

This study provides a thorough examination of the pedagogical beliefs held by pre-service teachers of mathematics, physics, chemistry, and biology, offering insights into the dominant perspectives on instructional dynamics. The research findings indicate that a substantial proportion of pre-service teachers hold teacher-centered beliefs, suggesting a notable preference for conventional educational paradigms. In contrast, a small proportion of participants hold student-centered beliefs, whereas a subset demonstrates a dual inclination towards both teacher- and student-centered orientations.

The analysis of subject domains highlights the differences in pedagogical beliefs among pre-service teachers. It is worth mentioning that teachers who specialize in physics education exhibit beliefs that prioritize the role of the teacher, with a clear tendency to place the teacher at the focal point of the educational environment. In the fields of chemistry and biology education, there is a significant presence of teacher-centered beliefs that can be observed. In contrast, the field of mathematics education displays a trend in which an equitable distribution becomes apparent. Roughly half of the pre-service teachers endorse the teacher-centered approach, while the other half align themselves with a student-centered perspective. The presence of this thought-provoking contrast within the field of mathematics education implies a sophisticated belief that simultaneously embraces both teacher-focused and student-focused approaches. It is apparent that pre-service teachers in various fields exhibit a dynamic interaction between different pedagogical perspectives, resulting in a complex combination of instructional approaches within the educational environment.

The findings of Markic and Eilks (2010) and Al-Amoush et al. (2011) provide further evidence of the widespread presence of conventional teacher-centered ideologies among educators. The concept of knowledge transfer from teacher to student, which is emphasized by teacher-centric viewpoints, is consistently observed and recorded in various research studies. In line with this theme, Elmas et al. (2011) present similar results in the context of chemistry educators, further confirming the prevalence of teacher-centered beliefs in the field of science education. Furthermore, the research carried out by Duban (2013) demonstrates a range of orientations observed among student teachers, with a significant portion leaning towards a middle ground position that incorporates aspects of both teacher-centered and student-centered approaches.

In the context of teaching styles, our study reveals a notable inclination towards the utilization of an explicit teaching style by pre-service teachers, which suggests a preference for a structured instructional approach. Interestingly, this approach is enhanced by a preference for a conceptual pedagogical approach, involving cooperative tasks, hands-on involvement, and intellectual discussions, as described by Thomas et al. (2001). In a similar vein, the research conducted by Bakir (2016) aligns with these results, indicating that most prospective science teachers demonstrate a blended instructional approach that combines elements of both teacher-centered and student-centered pedagogies. However, a small subset of individuals tends to lean towards an exploratory teaching methodology.

The study highlights the complex relationship between pedagogical beliefs and teaching styles in the context of pre-service teacher education. The various subtleties that have been observed provide evidence for the complex range of instructional approaches, underscoring the importance of developing a comprehensive comprehension of the diverse viewpoints that influence teaching methods.

5. Conclusion

This article concludes by highlighting the impact of teachers' beliefs on the teaching and learning of mathematics and science subjects. By categorizing these beliefs into traditional and contemporary approaches, we can gain a better understanding of how they influence the strategies, methods, and interactions used in the mathematics and in science classroom. In addition, the pyramid model illustrates the profound influence of beliefs on attitudes, decisions, and actions, offering educators who seek to improve their teaching practices valuable insights. As beliefs are deeply personal and difficult to alter, it is crucial to recognize their impact when designing mathematics and science teacher education environments that foster independent and meaningful student learning.

The study emphasizes the significance of systematic teacher education programs that target prospective teachers' beliefs and encourage ongoing critical reflection throughout their educational experience. Teacher professional development programs must provide opportunities for pre-service teachers to reassess and adjust their beliefs considering new perspectives. Furthermore, successful student-centered pedagogical techniques must be prioritized in teacher preparation programs. These programs can help pre-service teachers transition from traditional teaching methods to more learner-centered strategies. Teacher education programs influence and advance prospective teachers' beliefs by incorporating these perspectives, resulting in more effective and learner-focused teaching methods. In conclusion, the beliefs of teachers significantly impact their classroom practices and student career choices.

6. Recommendations

Further research in expanding the relationship between teacher beliefs and student career choices is needed. Categorizing teacher beliefs into teacher-centered and student-centered approaches as a result further provides valuable insights into their teaching strategies those teachers use in classroom. While many mathematics and science teachers tend to exhibit traditional, teacher-centered beliefs, teacher education programs must offer opportunities to reshape these beliefs toward more student-centered approaches. Understanding the influence of beliefs on teaching practices is essential for providing effective and student-centered science education. The findings of this study have significant implications for improving the overall quality of STEM education and equipping future educators with the necessary skills to address the changing needs of modern classrooms. Further research could explore additional factors that contribute to the formation and transformation of teachers' beliefs throughout their professional journey. The findings from this research can offer valuable insights into the factors influencing mathematics and science education in Kosovo and inform targeted interventions to enhance teaching and learning practices in the context of mathematics and science subjects.

References

Akkus, H. (2013). Pre-service secondary science teachers's images about themselves as a teacher. *Journal of Bactic Science Education*, 21(2), 249–260. https://doi.org/10.33225/jbse/13.12.249.

Al-Amoush, S. A., Markic, S., Abu-Hola, I., & Eilks, I. (2011). Jordanian prospective and experienced chemistry teachers' beliefs about teaching and learning and their potential role for educational reform. *Science Education International*, 22(3), 185–201.

Ambusaidi, A. K., & Al-Balushi, S. M. (2012). A longitudinal study to ıdentify prospective science teachers' beliefs about science teaching using the draw-a-science-teacher-test checklist. *International Journal of Environmental and Science Education*, 7(2), 291–311.

Bakir, S. (2016). What are their beliefs? What ıs their approach in practice? What ıs the profile of their science teachers and professors? *International Journal of Environmental and Science Education*, 11(5), 587–602.

Bandura, A. (1986). *Social foundations of thought and action*. Englewood Cliffs, NJ.

Boz, Y., & Uzuntiryaki, E. (2006). Turkish prospective chemistry teachers' beliefs about chemistry teaching. *International Journal of Science Education*, 28(14), 1647–1667. https://doi.org/10.1080/09500690500439132.

Bryan, L. A., & Abell, S. K. (1999). Development of professional knowledge in learning to teach elementary science. *Journal of Research in Science Teaching: The Official Journal of the National Association for Research in Science Teaching*, 36(2), 121–139. https://doi.org/10.1002/(SICI)1098-2736(199902)36:2<121::AID-TEA2>3.0.CO;2-U.

Deng, F., Chai, C. S., Tsai, C. C., & Lee, M. H. (2014). The relationships among Chinese practicing teachers' epistemic beliefs, pedagogical beliefs and their beliefs about the use of ICT. *Journal of Educational Technology & Society*, 17(2), 245–256.

Duban, N. Y. (2013). Pre-service science and technology teachers' mental images of science teaching. *Eurasian Journal of Educational Research*, 50, 107–126.

El Takach, S. (2018). How do early childhood education pre-service teachers view science and scientists? *The Eurasia Proceedings of Educational and Social Science*, 9, 104–119.

Elmas, R., Demirdöğen, B., & Geban, Ö. (2011). Preservice chemistry teachers' images about science teaching in their future classrooms. *Hacettepe University Journal of Education*, 40(40), 164–175.

Hancock, E. S., & Gallard, A. J. (2004). Preservice science teachers' beliefs about teaching and learning: The influence of K-12 field experiences. *Journal of Science Teacher Education*, 15(4), 281–291. https://doi.org/10.1023/B:JSTE.0000048331.17407.f5.

Leonard, J., Barnes-Johnson, J., Dantley, S. J., & Kimber, C. (2011). Teaching science inquiry in urban contexts: The role of elementary preservice teachers' beliefs. *The Urban Review*, 43, 124–150. https://doi.org/10.1007/s11256-010-0173-7.

Lin, H. L., Hazareesingh, N., Taylor, J., Gorrell, J., & Carlson, H. L. (2001). Early childhood and elementary preservice teachers' beliefs. *Journal of Early Childhood Teacher Education*, 22(3), 135–150. https://doi.org/10.1080/1090102010220302.

Mariani, L. (1999, March 18–20). *Probling the hidden curriculum: Teachers' and students beliefs and attitudes.* Retrieved February 2023, from The British Council 18th National Conference for Teachers of English: http://www.learningpaths.org/papers/paperbeliefs.htm

Markic, S., & Eilks, I. (2010). First-year science education student teachers' beliefs about student-and teacher-centerednes: Parallels and differences between chemistry and other science teaching domains. *Journal of Chemical Education*, 87(3), 335–339. https://doi.org/10.1021/ed8000864.

Markic, S., & Eilks, I. (2013). Potential changes in prospective chemistry teachers' beliefs about teaching and learning—A cross-level study. *International Journal of Science and Mathematics Education*, 11, 979–998. https://doi.org/10.1007/s10763-013-9417-9.

Markic, S., & Elliks, I. (2012). A comparison of student teachers' beliefs from four different science teaching domains using a mixed methods design. *International Journal of Science Education*, 34(4), 589–608. https://doi.org/10.1080/09500693.2011.608092.

Martin, J. D. (1997). *Elementary science methods: A constructivist approach.* USA: Delmar Publisher.

Mayer, R. E. (2003). Theories of learning and their application to technology. In H. F. O'Neil, Jr & R. S. Perez (Eds.), *Technology applications in education: A learning view* (pp. 127–157). Lawrence Erlbaum Associates Publishers.

Pajares, M. F. (1992). Teachers' beliefs and educational research: Cleaning up a Messy construct. *Review of Educational Research*, 62(3), 307–332. https://doi.org/10.3102/00346543062003307.

Porlán, R., & Del Pozo, R. M. (2004). The conceptions of in-service and prospective primary school teachers about the teaching and learning of science. *Journal of Science Teacher Education*, 15(1), 39–62. https://doi.org/10.1023/B:JSTE.0000031462.40615.56.

Saçıcı, S. (2013). *The interrelation between pre-service science teachers' conceptions of teaching and learning, learning approaches and self-efficacy beliefs.* Master's thesis: Middle East Technical University.

Savasci-Acikalin, F. (2009). Teacher beliefs and practice in science education. *Asia-Pacific Forum on Science Learning and Teaching*, 10(1), 1–14.

Schumacher, F., & Wilde, M. (2021). When prospective biology teachers visualize their beliefs about teaching and learning by drawing it, is it more than a reproduction of their experienced school lessons? *European Journal of Educational Research*, 10(2), 799–811. https://doi.org/10.12973/eu-jer.10.2.799.

Thomas, J. A., Pedersen, J. E., & Finson, K. (2001). Validating the Draw-A-Science-Teacher-Test Checklist (DASTT-C): Exploring mental models and teacher beliefs. *Journal of Science Teacher Education*, 12(4), 295–310. https://doi.org/10.1023/A:1014216328867.

Thomson, M. M., Turner, J. E., & Nietfeld, J. L. (2012). A typological approach to investigate the teaching career decision: Motivations and beliefs about teaching of prospective teacher candidates. *Teaching and Teacher Education*, 28(3), 324–335. https://doi.org/10.1016/j.tate.2011.10.007.

Tsai, C. C. (2002). Nested epistemologies: Science teachers' beliefs of teaching, learning and science. *International Journal of Science Education*, 24(8), 771–783. https://doi.org/10.1080/09500690110049132.

Whyte, A., & Ellis, N. (2003). Graphic representation as a bridge to understanding conceptual teaching. *Arts and Learning Research Journal*, 19(1), 167–194.

Yilmaz-Tuzun, O. (2008). Preservice elementary teachers' beliefs about science teaching. *Journal of Science Teacher Education*, 19(2), 183–204. https://doi.org/10.1007/s10972-007-9084-1.

Maija Zakrizevska-Belogrudova, Peteris Krasnikovs,
and Lucija Rutka

Teachers' Professional Stress Coping Strategies during COVID-19 Restrictions in Latvia

1. Introduction

Teachers in comprehensive schools are professionals whose working conditions changed very rapidly when the COVID-19 pandemic restrictions came into force in the spring of 2020. In Latvia, a government decree in the spring of 2020 moved school teaching to remote mode. The change had to be fully implemented by the end of the school year (June), and in September 2020, after six weeks of face-to-face teaching, a second decision was made to move all types of teaching to remote mode gradually.

Education was a sector that had to transition many professionals to teaching several large groups remotely quickly while trying to reach learning objectives and maintain programs, schedules, and other organizational and administrative responsibilities that are often an integral part of the teachers' work.

However, most teachers lacked the technical, digital, and pedagogical skills to ensure a smooth, uninterrupted distance learning process in March 2020. Moreover, in many cases, teachers and students faced a lack of technical resources, communication, digital tools, knowledge, or skills as they transitioned to distance learning (Schleicher, 2020; Latvian Ministry of Education and Science, 2021). "Almost no one could have foreseen or believed that this situation would arise, and the current COVID-19 situation is and will be a huge challenge and learning experience for all educators around the world" (Guzdial, 2020; Lehmann, 2020; cited in MacIntyre et al., 2020). The current situation can be described as "extraordinary online homeschooling".

All the issues teachers faced might have caused teachers to experience high-stress levels during the COVID-19 epidemic (Zewude et al., 2023). Moreover, common stressors for teachers include increased workload, time constraints, work-life imbalance, limited autonomy, significant additional administrative responsibilities, strained relationships with colleagues or school leadership, unclear roles or role conflict, emotional labor, difficulties implementing change, fear of losing control of the classroom, and fear of evaluation, among others (Mercer & Gregersen, 2020, cited in MacIntyre et al., 2020). In addition, teachers are under pressure to develop and manage online lessons, manage virtual classrooms, and assess student achievement while dealing with the previous common stressors mentioned before.

2. Literature Review

Coping strategies are conscious actions or thoughts that people use when facing a stressful or unpleasant situation. Moreover, one important feature of coping strategies is that they are a conscious and direct approach to solving the problem, in contrast to the defense mechanisms of the psyche (which are mostly unconscious) (American Psychological Association, 2018).

When reviewing Latvian literature about coping strategies, it is clear that the word coping has several interpretations, and both in scientific literature and in students' works, additional terms are used, such as "overcoming difficulties", "coping", "coping with", and "adaptation".

Richard Lazarus studied people's reactions to stress back in the 1960s, and he proposed that people's reactions to stress can be divided into three parts: initial appraisal (the individual's perceived threat to self), a secondary appraisal (individuals come to their senses and evaluate their possible responses to stress), and coping (during which a particular response is taken). Lazarus also pointed out that this process is often non-linear and emphasized how people's stress responses may change in different situations as the situation changes and called this situational stress response "coping" (Carver et al., 1989). In addition, another study found that although situational influences are important, it is reasonable to argue that people develop certain habits when responding to stressful situations and that these habits also determine how people respond to new situations, naming this response as dispositional coping (Carver et al., 1989).

Interestingly, there is a significant positive correlation between most dispositional and situational strategies, both for adaptive strategies (such as active coping, among others) and seeking emotional support. Moreover, a positive correlation was also found between avoidance strategies (such as venting emotions and using alcohol/drugs, among others) and distraction (Carver et al., 1989). For example, one adaptive active coping strategy is supervision. It should be noted that Latvia 2021 was a project to start supervision for all school, pre-school and university teachers. The Latvian National Encyclopaedia describes the process of supervision as follows: "supervision is a modern practical form of support for professionals, groups of professionals, teams or organizations, in which, after exploring the needs of the client or customer, formulating the purpose of supervision and mutual agreement, the supervision process finds concrete solutions to various problems, provides support and facilitates the learning process" (Martinsone & Zakriževska-Belogrudova, 2021).

When the study of coping as a stress response started, it was viewed as an interaction of mainly two factors: the person and the situation. However, George Bonanno (Bonanno & Burton, 2013) and colleagues suggested that two-factor theories that only describe the interaction between the person and the situation were incomplete and added a third factor, the person's ability to choose a coping strategy. Bonanno describes a person's ability to choose appropriate coping strategies as consisting of three components:

a) A person's sensitivity to the situational context.
b) The availability of different coping strategies.
c) The ability to respond to feedback.

In addition, a person's ability to adapt stress-coping strategies to their situational context can increase the positive impact of these strategies on their well-being (Cheng, Lau, & Chan, 2014; Sinha, Lacadie, Constable, & Seo, 2016). In further research on stress coping, Sarah Folkman divided all forms of stress coping into two groups based on the purpose of the effect: "problem-focused" or "emotion-focused" (Folkman & Lazarus, 1980). Problem-focused strategies are based on actions that solve a problem or change the source of stress. In contrast, emotion-focused strategies are based on actions that reduce, change, or manage the negative emotions caused by the situation (Folkman & Lazarus, 1980).

Nowadays, stress coping and emotion regulation are studied as separate phenomena, although the boundaries between stress coping and emotion regulation are somewhat blurred in the scientific literature. Contemporary research on the distinction between coping and emotion regulation describes coping as managing a stressful situation or one's stress response. In contrast, emotion regulation refers to attempts to influence one's or others' emotions, including the type, intensity, and duration. Furthermore, emotion regulation is more commonly described as a process that is continuous and can be both conscious (e.g., suppressing anger to maintain a good relationship with a significant other) and unconscious (e.g., averting one's gaze from an uncomfortable look) (Naragon-Gainey et al., 2017), and this differs from what coping is, as the stressful situation might not always be present.

Even if stress coping and emotion regulation concepts are semantically distinct, these psychological phenomena share common origins and similar manifestations (Stanton, 2011, cited in Naragon-Gainey et al., 2017). Similar to coping strategies for stress, emotion regulation can be adaptive or maladaptive and have positive or negative relationships, respectively, with an individual's psychological, emotional, and physical well-being (Aldao et al., 2010; Gross, 2015; Wells, 2011; Naragon-Gainey et al., 2017).

Recently, it has been suggested that emotion management and problem-solving coping strategies are simultaneously activated in individuals under stress (Boniwell & Tunariu, 2019, cited in MacIntyre et al., 2020), and applying stress-coping strategies is crucial in managing stress, particularly in stressful occupations. For example, evidence-based strategies such as mindfulness, stress management training, and cognitive-behavioral interventions effectively reduced stress levels in the study participants. Additionally, engaging in healthy coping strategies such as physical activity and practicing stress-coping skills are essential in managing occupational stress. The development and routine practice of stress-coping strategies are necessary for individuals in high-stress occupations (Cahill et al., 2020). Moreover, strategies such as physical exercise, talking to others, mindfulness, and creating a calm work environment help manage stress and promote overall well-being (Díaz-Silveira et al., 2020).

Given the importance of stress-coping strategies and emotional responses, it becomes evident that these elements are crucial in managing occupational stress. As teachers worldwide had to adapt and respond to the unprecedented challenges that emerged from the COVID-19 pandemic, it is necessary to study the full extent of the coping and emotional responses by teachers used during this period (and afterward) and hopefully provide them with the necessary tools they need to reduce the stress attached to their profession and the new challenges faced.

3. Research Methodology

The study investigated teachers' coping strategies during COVID-19 constraints, when a distance learning mode was abruptly implemented, and to evaluate if the age, years of teaching experience, and experience with supervision influence the coping strategies used.

The data was collected exclusively through a survey and the research questions were:

1. What are the stress-coping strategies of teachers under COVID-19 constraints?
2. What are the relationships among teachers' stress coping strategies?
3. Are there differences in teachers' stress-coping strategies according to age and seniority?
4. Is there a relationship between stress-coping strategies and teachers' supervision experience?
5. Does attending supervision have an effect on stress management?

3.1. Sample Selection and Data Collection

The selection of respondents was done by (a) sending an invitation to complete the survey to publicly accessible e-mails in comprehensive schools and state gymnasiums, (b) snowball sampling, which is a method of selecting respondents based on the recommendations of others. According to the Central Statistical Office of the Republic of Latvia (2021), the gender distribution among general education teachers is 88 % female and 12 % male, so the gender difference in stress coping strategies was not investigated.

Before filling in the questionnaire, information was provided about the study, the authors of the study, that participation in the study was anonymous and voluntary, that the questionnaire was intended for teachers and educators, the purpose of the questionnaire, the structure of the questionnaire, and that the data collected would be used only in aggregate form. It also indicated the approximate time required to complete the survey, contact information in case of questions, and that by completing and submitting the survey, the participant agreed to participate in the study Survey data were processed using IBM SPSS version 22.

3.2. Variables

Supervision is the independent variable, and the dependent variables are the use of a given coping strategy and the efficiency of said coping strategies in reducing the teachers' stress levels.

He dependent variable is the use of a coping strategies. The coping strategies studied were:Active coping, Planning, Suppression of competing activities, Restraint coping, Seeking social support for instrumental reasons, Seeking social support for emotional reasons, Positive reinterpretation and growth, Acceptance, Turning to religion, Focus on recognizing and venting of emotions, Denial, Behavioral disengagement, Mental disengagement, Alcohol-drug disengagement Humor (COPE; Carver et al., 1989; adapted into Latvian by updated by V. Perepjolkina et al., 2020).

3.3. Method

The Coping Orientation of Problem Experience Inventory was used for data collection (COPE; Carver et al., 1989; adapted into Latvian by I. Petrova, 2009, LU; S. Knipše, 2010, LU; updated by V. Perepjolkina et al., 2020). The COPE questionnaire is a self-report instrument that identifies the source of stress a person faces and the coping strategies that person prefers in everyday life when faced with difficulties and stressful situations. The COPE questionnaire consists of sixty statements with four response options:

1. I almost never do it.
2. I rarely do it.
3. I often do it.
4. I almost always do it.

The respondent was asked to rate each statement and tick the appropriate response. The questionnaire is designed to be used both individually and frontally in a group. There is no time limit for completing the questionnaire, which takes ten to fifteen minutes to complete. The questionnaire is designed for adults (eighteen years and older). Both a generic and a situational version of the questionnaire are available. The general form is usually used for research purposes, but for individual consultations, both or only the situational form is used. The situational form was used in this study, asking participants to think about and respond to the difficulties the COVID-19 pandemic has caused at work. The situational form was designed to find out what coping tactics (strategies) people had used to deal with the situation and how they dealt with a particular situation. The questionnaire consists of fifteen scales (coping strategies):

1. Active coping.
2. Planning.
3. Suppression of competing activities.
4. Restraint coping.
5. Seeking social support for instrumental reasons.
6. Seeking social support for emotional reasons.
7. Positive reinterpretation and growth.
8. Acceptance.
9. Turning to religion.
10. Focus on and venting of emotions.
11. Denial.
12. Behavioral disengagement.
13. Mental disengagement.
14. Alcohol-drug disengagement.
15. Humor.

In addition, questions regarding the respondents' experience of supervision were added, and the aim was to collect their beliefs and perceptions about supervision. In addition, Data was collected about the participants' gender, age, and years of professional experience. An open-ended question, "How do you cope with stress?" was included so participants provide more context.

4. Findings and Discussion

The results of the Kolmogorov-Smirnov test show that the questionnaire scales used in the study show statistically significant differences between the empirical and theoretical distributions ($p < 0.05$). Therefore, the responses do not follow a normal distribution, and nonparametric statistical methods should be used for further data processing. The reliability of the scales ranges between 0.51 and 0.91.

4.1. Mean Values of Types of Coping Strategies in the Study Sample

Table 1: Coping strategies types

Type of Coping Strategies	M	SD
Adaptive strategies	10.97	1.30
Avoidance strategies	7.10	1.46
Neutral strategies	1.92	0.64

The coping strategies were grouped into adaptive, avoidant (non-adaptive), and neutral (Table 1). Adaptive strategies included active coping, Planning, suppression of competing activities, restraint coping, seeking social support for instrumental reasons, seeking social support for emotional reasons, positive reinterpretation and growth, and acceptance. On the other hand, avoidance strategies include focusing on and venting emotions, denial, behavioral disengagement, mental disengagement, and alcohol-drug disengagement. Finally, the neutral strategies were turning to religion and Humor.

This study shows similar results to another study (Carver et al., 1989). However, there were major differences in several strategies (mean values of the scales of the Stress Coping Strategies Questionnaire). For example, the use of Mental Disengagement and Humor greatly increased (from 1.4 to 9.2 and from 3.2 to 7.5, respectively). In contrast, the Alcohol-Drug Disengagement strategy was significantly reduced (from 8.8 to 5.2) (Carver et al., 1989).

Nevertheless, the Alcohol-drug disengagement strategy was still significantly higher among teachers compared to other professionals, suggesting a possible link with the COVID-19 situation. It seems that teachers use distractions, turn to other activities, and deny or minimize the importance of the problem through Humor to relieve tension. Alcohol and drug use shows the lowest value of all the strategies and indicates that alcohol use for stress is not very common among teachers. Teachers use less alcohol for stress reduction than the national average (28 %) (Kantar, 2018).

In addition to analyzing the most used coping strategies, a correlation analysis between the scales was carried out to examine if there were relations between the different coping strategies. As the questionnaire scales do not follow a normal distribution, Spearman's rank correlation coefficient was used to calculate the correlations between the scales (Table 2).

Table 2: Correlations between stress management strategies

Stress Management Strategy	Active Coping	Planning	Suppression of Competing Activities	Seeking Social Support for Instrumental Reasons	Focus on and Venting of Emotions	Denial
Planning	0.62	–				
Suppression of competing activities	0.31	0,44	–			
Seeking social support for instrumental reasons	0.37	0.51	0.33	–		
Seeking social support for emotional reasons	0.28	0.28	0.28	0.65		
Behavioral disengagement		-0.15	0.32		0.42	0.43

As can be seen in Table 2, several moderate and strong correlations have been found. Active coping positively correlated with Planning (0.62; $p < 0.001$). In addition, Planning was positively correlated with seeking social support for instrumental reasons (0.51; $p < 0.001$), and the former correlated with seeking social support for emotional reasons (0.65; $p < 0.001$).

Table 3: Mean values of stress coping strategies in different age groups

Stress Management Strategy	Average Rank Values by Age Group			Kruskal-Wallis Test Result	Bilateral Level of Relevance
	23–40 years N = 39 22 %	41–60 years N = 109 61 %	61–75 years N = 31 17,3 %		
Active coping	74.5	100.4	105.0	6.3	0.042**
Turning to religion	72.1	92.1	90.8	6.3	0.042**
Focus on & venting of emotions	102.0	96.0	71.1	6.4	0.041**
Humor	112.2	90.7	59.7	18.1	0.000**

Afterward, a Rank analysis of variance (Kruskal-Wallis test) was used to examine differences in coping strategies between age and tenure groups (Tables 3 and 4). As can be seen in Table 3, Humor was significantly less used as a coping strategy in both the 41–60 and 61–75 age groups compared to the 23–40 age group ($p < 0.001$). Moreover, all four strategies shown in Table 3 significantly differ between age groups ($p < 0.001$).

Table 4: Mean values of stress coping strategies in seniority groups

Stress Management Strategy	Average Rank Values Seniority Groups				Kruskal-Wallis Test Result	Bilateral Level of Relevance
	0,5–5 years N = 26 15 %	6–20 years N = 53 30 %	21–35 years N = 76 42 %	36–51 years N = 24 13 %		
Planning	91.4	71.3	101.2	94.3	10.9	0.012*
Turning to religion	61.1	93.1	94.4	101.1	10.4	0.016*
Humor	116.0	108.2	74.3	71.3	23.6	0.000**

When comparing the coping strategies between the seniority groups, three strategies showed significant differences between the groups: Planning (10.9; $p < 0.05$), Turning to religion (10.4; $p <0.05$), and humor (23.6; $p < 0.000$) (Table 4). It can be seen that Humor was mostly used by teachers who belonged to the 0.5–5 years of experience group and that there was a continued decrease in the use of Humor when the years of experience were higher. In contrast, Turning to religion follows the opposite trend, as its use is directly proportional to teachers' years of experience (4).

Table 5: Differences in coping strategies for respondents with or without supervisory experience

Stress Management Strategy	**Average Rank Values**		**Mann - Vit U Test Result**	**Bilateral Level of Relevance**
	Supervisor Experience N = 85	**No supervisor experience N = 94**		
Active coping	100.56	80.45	-2.64	0.008**

On the other hand, a Spearman's rank correlation analysis was conducted (Table 2). In order to determine whether there are differences in stress-coping strategies between teachers with and without supervisor experience, a Mann-Whitney test was conducted to compare two independent samples (Table 5). The results showed a statistically significant difference in one coping strategy—active coping (-2.64, $p < 0.01$).

In this study, nearly half of the teachers surveyed (47 %) have had at least one supervision experience, and most (92 %) have heard of or know what supervision is. The results show a statistically significant difference in one coping strategy—*active coping* (-2.64, $p < 0.01$). These results suggest that teachers with supervision experience were more likely to engage in active stress management than teachers without supervision experience. In addition, the strategies of seeking social support—for instrumental and emotional purposes—and positive reappraisal of the experience showed a positive relationship with attitudes toward supervision, suggesting that teachers who had supervision experience might have been better prepared or trained on how to reduce stress and are more likely to turn to colleagues for advice or support daily and reappraise their experiences. Consequently, teachers' beliefs about the usefulness of supervision are positively related to adaptive coping strategies in general.

To answer the research question: does attending supervision have an impact on coping with stress, a linear regression ANOVA was performed. The data analysis shows that attending supervision does not have an impact on coping.

Our findings align with previous studies highlighting the positive effects of supervision for teachers. Supervision helps teachers identify and practice positive teaching behaviors, enhancing their level of teaching and effectively engaging students in the classroom (Levine, 2011). Supervision also provides teachers with feedback that enables them to identify areas for improvement and develop strategies to enhance their teaching effectiveness (Purba & Parhusip, 2023). Additionally, instructional supervision has been found to have a dominant effect on variations in learning models and teacher learning materials in schools (Kraft et al., 2018). Furthermore, research shows that implementing academic supervision positively correlates with improving teachers' performance (Uju 2017). These findings indicate that supervision is crucial in fostering teachers' professional development and enhancing student learning outcomes.

5. Conclusion

Teachers in the COVID-19 context mostly used adaptive cognitive coping strategies to deal with professional stress. Generally, teachers in the COVID-19 setting used more adaptive strategies than neutral or avoidant ones to cope with professional stress. Therefore, it can be concluded that most teachers in the COVID-19 setting were likely to cope with stress at work by reevaluating the current situation, trying to see and find something useful in it, being proactive, planning, and communicating with colleagues and friends.

Active coping showed a positive, strong relationship with planning as well as other scales. Planning showed a relationship with seeking social support for instrumental reasons. In addition, seeking social support for instrumental reasons correlated with seeking social support for emotional reasons.

When examining the differences in teacher age and seniority groups, it was found that there are differences between teachers aged 23–40 and 41–60 in the strategies of active coping and Turning to religion. Both strategies are less pronounced in the 23–40 group compared to the 41–60 group. In contrast, focusing on emotions and using Humor are more used in the 23–40 age group than in the 41–60 age group

It can, therefore, be concluded that some strategies are more pronounced in young teachers, which can be explained by less experience, while some emotion-focused strategies are less pronounced in older teachers, which might derive from being more knowledgeable and experienced.

The results of the study show that there is a relationship between active stress management and teachers with supervisory experience. Teachers' positive attitudes towards supervision are positively related to seeking support for instrumental and emotional purposes and positive reappraisal. Overall, teachers' positive attitudes toward supervision are consistent with adaptive strategies, suggesting that teachers who tend to be active problem solvers, seek and provide support and assistance to colleagues, learn, and reevaluate their experiences are also more likely to participate in supervision and see the benefits of it.

References

Aldao, A., & Nolen-Hoeksema, S. (2010). The influence of context on the implementation of adaptive emotion regulation strategies. *Behavior Research and Therapy,* 50(7–8), 493–501. https://doi.org/10.1016/j.brat.2012.04.0047, https://doi.org/10.1037/bul0000093.

American Psychological Association. (2018). *Coping strategy.* Retrieved from: https://dictionary.apa.org/coping-strategy

Aslakson, A. J., Melton, B. F., Bland, H. W., & Biber, D. D. (2023). Physical activity solutions to decrease occupational stress. *ACSM's Health and Fitness Journal,* 27(3), 33–40: American College of Sports Medicine. doi: https://doi.org/10.1249/FIT.0000000000000864.

Bonanno, G. A., & Burton, C. L. (2013). Regulatory flexibility: An individual differences perspective on coping and emotion regulation. *Perspectives on Psychological Science: A Journal of the Association for Psychological Science,* 8(6), 591–612. https://doi.org/10.1177/1745691613504116.

Boniwell, I., & Tunariu, A. D. (2019). *Positive psychology: Theory, research and applications* (2nd ed.). Open University Press.

Cahill, J., Cullen, P., Anwer, S., Wilson, S., & Gaynor, K. (2021). Pilot Work Related Stress (WRS), effects on wellbeing and mental health, and coping methods. *The International Journal of Aerospace Psychology,* 31(2), 87–109. https://doi.org/10.1080/24721840.2020.1858714.

Central Statistical Office of the Republic of Latvia. (2021). *Dzimumu līdztiesība: izglītība un zinātne.* [Gender equality: education and science]. Retrieved from: https://stat.gov.lv/lv/statistikas-temas/labklajibas-un-vienlidzibas-raditaji/dzimumlidztiesiba/6301-dzimumu-lidztiesiba?themeCode=GE

Cheng, C., Lau, H.-P. B., & Chan, M.-P. S. (2014). Coping flexibility and psychological adjustment to stressful life changes: A meta-analytic review. *Psychological Bulletin,* 140(6), 1582–1607. https://doi.org/10.1037/a0037913.

Díaz-Silveira, C., Alcover, C. M., Burgos, F., Marcos, A., & Santed,M. A. (2020). Mindfulness versus physical exercise: Effects of two recovery strategies on mental health, stress and immunoglobulin a during lunch breaks: A randomized controlled trial. *International Journal of Environmental Research and Public Health,* 20; 17(8), 2839. https://doi.org/10.3390/ijerph17082839. PMID: 32326082; PMCID: PMC7215846.

Folkman, S., & Lazarus, R. S. (1980). An analysis of coping in a middle-aged community sample. *Journal of Health and Social Behavior,* 21(3), 219–239. https://doi.org/10.2307/2136617.

Gross, J. J. (2015). Emotion regulation: Current status and future prospects. *Psychological Inquiry,* 26(1), 1–26. https://doi.org/10.1080/1047840x.2014.940781

Guzdial, M. (2020). So much to learn about emergency remote teaching, but so little to claim about online learning. *Computing Education Research Blog.* Retrieved from https://computinged.wordpress.com/2020/03/30/so-much-to-learn-about-emergency-remote-teaching-but-so-little-to-claim-about-online-learning/. Accessed on: (2023).

Kraft, M. A., Blazar, D., & Hogan, D. (2018). The effect of teacher coaching on instruction and achievement: A meta-analysis of the causal evidence. *Review of Educational Research,* 88(4), 547–588. https://doi.org/10.3102/0034654318759268.

Latvian Ministry of Education and Science. (2021). Pētījuma "Attālināto mācību pirmās 2 nedēļas" rezultātu kopsavilkums. [Summary of the results of the study The first 2 weeks of distance learning]. Retrieved from: https://home.edurio.com/izm-attalinato-macibu-rezultati

Lehmann, C. (2020). "Doing School" In The Time of Coronavirus – Practical Theory. Practical Theory. Retrieved from: https://practicaltheory.org/blog/2020/03/26/doing-school-in-the-time-of-coronavirus/ Accessed on: 2023.

Levine, T. H. (2011). Features and strategies of supervisor professional community as a means of improving the supervision of preservice teachers. *Teaching and Teacher Education,* 27(5), 930–941. https://doi.org/10.1016/j.tate.2011.03.004.

MacIntyre, P. D., Gregersen, T., & Mercer, S. (2020). Language teachers' coping strategies during the Covid-19 conversion to online teaching: Correlations with stress, wellbeing and negative emotions. *System,* 94, 102352. https://doi.org/10.1016/j.system.2020.102352.

Mārtinsone, K., & Zakriževska-Belogrudova, M. (2021). Supervīzija. [Supervision]. *Latvian National Encyclopedia: Supervision.* Retrieved from: https://enciklopedija.lv/skirklis/98499-superv%C4%ABzija. Accessed on: 2023.

Naragon-Gainey, K., McMahon, T. P., & Chacko, T. P. (2017). The structure of common emotion regulation strategies: A meta-analytic examination. *Psychological Bulletin,* 143(4), 384–424.

Perepjolkina, V., Koļesņikova, J., Mārtinsone, K., & Stepens, A. (2020). *Latvijas klīniskais personības tests: Tehniskā rokasgrāmata.* [Latvia's clinical personality test: Technical manual.]. Rīga: Rīgas Stradiņa universitāte (p. 463). [Riga: Riga's Stradiņa University]. *Kantar TNS (2018), pētījums par aktuāliem ar darbu un darba tirgu saistītiem jautājumiem.* [Research on current issues related to work and the labor market.]. Retrieved from: https://www.kantar.lv/newsletters/tnsab55/darbinieku-vidu-iezimejas-profesionalas-izdegsanas-problema/. Accessed on: 2023.

Purba, S., & Parhusip, A. (2023). Enhancing the Paikem learning model's applicability: The clinical supervision model. *Edunesia: Jurnal Ilmiah Pendidikan*, 4(2), 631–643. https://doi.org/10.51276/edu.v4i2.427

Sinha, R., Lacadie, C. M., Constable, R. T., & Seo, D. (2016). Dynamic neural activity during stress signals resilient coping. *Proc Natl Acad Sci U S A*,113(31), 8837–42. doi: 10.1073/pnas.1600965113.

Schleicher, A. (2020). *The impact of Covid-19 on education: Insights from education at a glance* (2020). Retrieved from: https://www.oecd.org/education/the-impact-of-covid-19-on-education-insights-education-at-a-glance-2020.pdf

Uju, F. E., & Paul, A O. (2017). Enhancing the standard of teaching and learning in the 21st century via qualitative school-based supervision in secondary schools in Abuja municipal area council (AMAC). *International Journal of Educational Administration and Policy Studies*, 9(6), 79–83. https://doi.org/10.5897/ijeaps2016.0490.

Wells, A. (2011). *Metacognitive therapy for anxiety and depression*. Guilford Press.

Zewude, G. T., Beyene, S. D., Taye, B., Sadouki, F., & Hercz, M. (2023). COVID-19 stress and teachers well-being: The mediating role of sense of coherence and resilience. *European Journal of Investigation in Health, Psychology and Education*, 13, 1–22. https://doi.org/10.3390/ejihpe13010001.

Mislav Ante Omazić

Educating through Personal Transformation: The Impact of a Change Management Course on Students and the Community through Service Learning

1. Introduction: Transforming Theory into Practice

"This course has been a game-changer for me. Initially, I thought managing long-term projects wasn't my thing, but after I finished, I must admit that I was wrong. We're not just learning theory here; we're applying it to real-life stuff, which is pretty cool. Setting SMARTER goals was new to me—focusing not just on the practical side but also on making sure our goals are ethically sound, and doable with what we have. I've learned a ton about working in a team, like how everyone's skills are important and how to pull it all together. Sure, it's been tough at times, balancing everything, but I've picked up skills I know I'll use way beyond university—like how to stay on track with big projects and make decisions that aren't just about ticking boxes, but actually mean something. It's been more than just another class for me—it's been about getting ready for the real world, and that's pretty exciting. In the end, I didn't care about a grade because I did get much more than a number". This quotation summarizes the overall experience of students after going through meaningful socially responsible projects and taking a "Change Management" course.

The course employs a team-based project approach, engaging students in developing and executing socially responsible initiatives, effectively linking academic theory with real-world practice. As written by Resch and Schrittesser (2023), this innovative educational approach integrates service learning with real-world applications, significantly enhancing undergraduate students' learning experiences and bridging the gap between academic theory and practice. The course's impact extends beyond the classroom, with tangible contributions made to societal issues, reflecting a successful model of integrating service learning into higher education. This chapter aims to shed light on the course's approach and its effectiveness in preparing undergraduate students for both professional and societal challenges.

Service learning as a method fosters civic responsibility and prepares students for professional challenges, providing impactful and memorable community immersion experiences (Omar et al., 2022). Incorporating service learning into the curriculum, education becomes more interactive and engaging, allowing students to practically apply their academic knowledge. This holistic approach not only makes learning hands-on but also enriches community service, resulting in a transformative educational experience that benefits both students and the wider community. Furthermore, service learning helps to bridge the gap between theoretical knowledge and real-world application, fostering critical thinking and problem-solving skills essential for future careers (Jones, 2001). By actively participating in community projects, students develop a sense of social responsibility and gain a deeper understanding of societal issues, thus preparing them to become informed and engaged citizens (Bringle & Hatcher, 2009).

2. From Theory to Action: Service-Learning as a Catalyst for Experiential Education

Service-learning, grounded in experiential learning and John Dewey's educational philosophy, emphasizes active participation over passive learning. It has emerged as a key focus in education, promoting hands-on experiences. Dewey, in his seminal work (1938), argued that education is most effective when it is connected to real-life situations, enabling students to apply theoretical knowledge to practical experiences. According to Maddux and Donnett (2015), Dewey's principles of inquiry mandate that educators create situations that challenge students' assumptions, encouraging them to critically examine their beliefs and engage deeply with the material. This concept is further developed in David Kolb's Experiential Learning Theory (ELT), which posits that knowledge is constructed through a cycle of concrete experiences, reflective observation, abstract conceptualization, and active experimentation (Kolb, 1984). This cycle underscores learning as a continuous, dynamic process where the learner actively engages in interpreting and reinterpreting experiences, thereby shaping their perception of the world and their role in it (Healey & Jenkins, 2000; Schön, 1992).

Dewey's and Kolb's theories highlight learning as an interactive, transformative journey, shifting the focus of education from mere knowledge transmission to fostering critical thinking, problem-solving, and application of knowledge in various contexts. Service-learning, as a form of experiential education, is rooted in cognitive and developmental psychology, pragmatic philosophy, and democratic theory (Morton & Troppe, 1996).

Defining service learning is complex as it does not adhere to a single, straightforward definition. This educational approach draws from a variety of intellectual traditions and value systems, which often appear to be in contradiction or competition with each other. Service learning is grounded in the principle that real-life experience is vital for learning, using community service as a practical foundation. As seen in picture 1 service-learning, as an educational approach, embodies on a voluntary basis these principles by combining academic learning objectives and practical experience with community service. Service-learning, a practical application of this theory, intertwines community service with academic study to enrich learning, teach civic responsibility, and strengthen communities (Bringle & Hatcher, 1996; Simsek, 2020). This integration allows students to apply classroom theories to practical scenarios, thereby enriching their learning experience and fostering a deeper understanding of the subject matter (Omar et al., 2022). The experiential nature of service-learning aligns perfectly with Dewey's and Kolb's emphasis on learning through experience, reinforcing the idea that education should be an engaging, active, and socially relevant process.

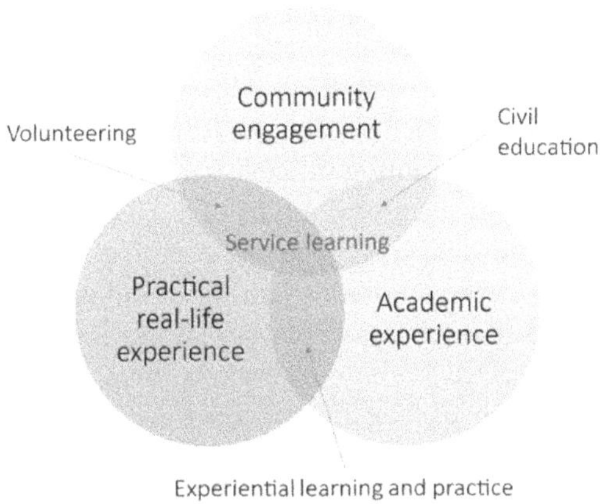

Figure 1: Service-learning at the intersection of theory and practice

The Figure 1 illustrates the integration of three core aspects of service learning: community engagement, practical real-life experience, and academic experience. At the center of these overlapping circles is "Service Learning," highlighting how it combines elements of volunteering, civil education, and experiential learning to create a comprehensive educational approach. This intersection emphasizes that service learning not only enhances academic learning through practical application but also fosters community involvement and personal growth. By merging these components, service learning provides a holistic and transformative educational experience, preparing students for professional and civic responsibilities. A core principle of service-learning is reciprocity, which refers to the mutually beneficial relationship between the student and the community. It's not just about students providing service on a voluntary basis; it's equally about what they learn from the experience. This reciprocal model ensures that both parties benefit: communities receive valuable services for free, while students gain practical skills and insights that enhance their academic and personal growth (Stanton, Giles & Cruz., 1999; Simsek, 2020). Reciprocity in service-learning fosters a deeper understanding of societal issues, encouraging students to reflect on their role in the community and the impact of their contributions.

3. Service-Learning: Bridging Academia and Community through Reciprocal Education

By integrating service learning into the curriculum, students are enabled to apply their academic knowledge in real-life environments, facilitating the translation of theoretical knowledge into practical skills (Carver, 1997; Dedehouanou, 2022). Additionally, this approach benefits the community, with students directly addressing local needs while gaining valuable hands-on experience.

As seen in picture 2 this reciprocal model of learning ensures that education goes beyond mere knowledge acquisition, focusing instead on making a tangible difference in society and contributing to individual competencies by implementing theoretical models into practice. It illustrates the interconnected elements essential to service learning. It features three overlapping circles: one representing collaborative partnerships focused on contextual solutions and problems, another for the practical application of acquired knowledge and skills through teamwork, and the third highlighting reflection and self-assessment for deeper individual understanding. At the center, where these circles overlap, is "Service Learning," indicating that effective service learning integrates collaboration, practical application, and reflective practice to benefit both students and communities. This model underscores the reciprocal nature of service learning, where mutual benefit and deeper engagement are achieved through these combined efforts. Such a model could serve as an exemplary blueprint for academic institutions aiming to create a dynamic and relevant learning environment, producing graduates who are adept at navigating and contributing positively to an ever-evolving global landscape (Mason & Dunens, 2019; Dedehouanou, 2022). The integration of service-learning into curriculum design involves a deliberate alignment of academic objectives with community needs, creating a mutually beneficial educational experience. Faculty play a crucial role in this integration, as they must design course content that not only meets academic standards but also addresses real-world challenges faced by community partners (Furco, 1996). This intentional design is vital for ensuring that service-learning goes beyond volunteerism, embedding it deeply within the educational objectives of the course (Figure 2).

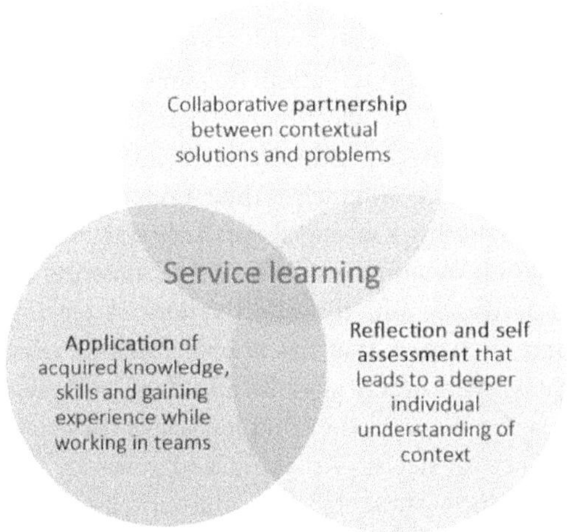

Figure 2: Reciprocal model of service learning

Effective service-learning implementation necessitates faculty training, suitable community partnerships, and alignment with institutional goals (Jacoby, 2015). It also requires ongoing assessment to measure the impact on both students and the community. This assessment helps in refining the service-learning experiences to maximize benefits and address any challenges that arise (Eyler, Giles & Astin, 1999).

As educational institutions continue to embrace this approach, it becomes increasingly important to understand and refine its implementation strategies to ensure that it remains a powerful tool for learning and community engagement.

4. Shaping Future Leaders: Nurturing Practical Skills and Civic Responsibility through Service-Learning

Aligned with the university's mission of practical learning and community engagement, the elective course provides a unique educational experience.

Integrating practical applications into the curriculum, it addresses a gap commonly found in traditional teaching methods. Aiming to deepen students' understanding of change management principles, the course applies these concepts in real-world scenarios. Achieving this objective involves a curriculum restructuring to emphasize practical elements, thus facilitating the development and execution of socially responsible projects.

The projects undertaken by students span a wide range of themes, addressing essential societal challenges and community needs. These include social support for marginalized groups, issues related to the elderly, community belonging, food access, language and cultural preservation, housing, urban development, refugee support and social integration, environmental conservation, waste management, and deforestation. These diverse projects enable students to apply academic theories to practical settings, enhancing their understanding of various global and local issues, and fostering a strong sense of civic responsibility.

The course's design is dynamic and responsive, evolving each academic year based on student feedback and the effectiveness of teaching methods. This continuous adaptation ensures that the course remains relevant and effective in providing students with practical skills and deep comprehension of change management, preparing them for the complexities of the professional world and instilling values of ethical decision-making and resource utilization. Through this hands-on experience, students gain a comprehensive understanding of managing change, contributing to their personal and professional development. This hands-on experience solidifies their understanding of the complexities involved in managing change. Moreover, the course is designed as a dynamic, evolving entity. Based on feedback from students and the observed effectiveness of teaching methods, innovations and improvements are introduced each academic year, such as:

1. Mentorship has emerged as a fundamental component of educational curricula, playing a crucial role in the successful learning experiences of students in higher education (Santora, Mason & Sheahan, 2013; Foster, Ooms & Marks-Maran, 2015; Arnesson & Albinsson, 2017; Nuis, Segers & Beausaert, 2023). Allen, Poteet, and Burroughs (1997) emphasize the significance of mentorship in enhancing students' academic and professional development. That is why for this course, a mentor base of 25–30 individuals was developed and regularly revised. The list includes a diverse range of professional profiles, from managers and entrepreneurs to individuals working in non-profit organizations and public figures. Each year, the list is reviewed, and all mentors are contacted before the commencement of the course to confirm their availability and willingness to dedicate time to student projects. On average, mentors meet with the project teams 1–2 times during the project execution. Ragins and Kram (2007) suggest that effective mentorship can lead to increased confidence

and skill development in students. During these meetings, mentors provide advice on enhancing the project and assist in overcoming obstacles. It is crucial to note that mentors are instructed not to be part of the project team and that the realization of project goals is not their responsibility.

At the inception of this initiative, it was observed that students were hesitant to utilize mentors in their project execution, particularly due to the public recognition of the mentors involved. This hesitancy underscores the importance of fostering a positive mentor-student relationship, which has been highlighted as crucial in various studies (Hudson, 2013; Sarabipour et al., 2022; Nuis, Segers, & Beausaert, 2023). Emphasizing the mentor-student-teacher relationship is crucial for the success of projects and the professional growth of students in this course. Such an approach guarantees the course's relevance, contemporaneity, and responsiveness to evolving needs.

2. Generally, one of the most common reasons for team motivation loss is the free-rider effect. When students work in teams, there's a tendency for certain members to contribute less effort, relying on others to carry the workload, a behaviour known as "free-riding." They work less because they're counting on the compassion of their colleagues and know that they will compensate and complete the task for them. This issue is particularly pronounced in academic environments where collective assessment is employed, and students do have to perform in teams. Kerr and Bruun (1983) have extensively discussed how individual contributions can become less noticeable in group settings, leading to decreased effort from some members. In addition, social loafing, may occur when that type of team member cannot be identified, meaning there are no rewards or punishments for them.

   In addition to what has been previously written, students are encouraged to continuously evaluate the contributions of other team members and to take responsibility if they notice undesirable behaviour from peers during the project. Therefore, students can send an email to instructors, highlighting specific instances of such behaviour and including all other team members in the email. Subsequently, a meeting is convened to discuss the possibility of their continued participation in the team. Over the past decade, there have been several such situations where almost always those team members whose performance was not satisfactory to others, peacefully exited the team and took responsibility. Likewise, at the end of the course, students also evaluate each other. All of this aims to encourage students to make "tough" decisions if they do not want to tolerate the indolence of their colleagues.

   Aggarwal and O'Brien (2008) have explored how the structure of group projects can influence the extent of social loafing, suggesting that clear individual accountability and task interdependence can mitigate this issue. So, there is an obvious need for educators to implement measures that ensure equitable participation and responsibility in team-based assignments, thereby reducing the occurrence of free-riding and enhancing the overall effectiveness of group learning. Therefore, one of the first assignments that students, who are randomly selected in teams of 4–6 members, have on the Change management course is a group assignment where they evoke previous positive and negative experiences of working in teams and they define a clear set of rules they agree to follow. This exercise not only encourages reflection and learning from past experiences but also fosters a sense of ownership and commitment towards the team's objectives. By establishing agreed-upon norms and responsibilities from the outset, teams can function more cohesively, ensuring that each member contributes meaningfully to the project. This initial step is crucial in building a foundation for effective collaboration and accountability, setting the stage for more successful and engaging group work throughout the course. Additionally, the continuous evaluation and responsibility-taking mechanisms encourage students to confront and address indolence within the team, fostering a culture of accountability and proactive problem-solving.

3. This course also emphasizes the importance of continuous work and responsibility among students. This is particularly relevant for newer generations who might struggle with maintaining a long-term focus on tasks (Kirschner & Karpinski, 2010; Rosen Carrier & Cheever, 2013; Chen & Yan, 2016; Allison, 2020). Zimmerman (2002) highlights the necessity of self-regulated learning for academic success, a principle that the course integrates by basing part of the student's grades on the achievement of project goals, presentation of results, peer evaluation of team contributions, and the submission of weekly reports. These weekly reports encourage students to reflect on their accomplishments and plan for the upcoming week, fostering the breakdown of large projects into smaller, manageable tasks. Each task is assigned a lead, deadline, and specific outcomes, aligning with SMART criteria for goal setting (Doran, 1981; Bjerke & Renger, 2017), which focuses on creating specific, measurable, achievable, relevant, and time-bound objectives. This approach teaches students to take ownership of their tasks and to coordinate effectively with their peers, fostering essential skills such as time management, organization, and teamwork.

   Furthermore, the course extends the SMART framework to SMARTER goals, where 'E' stands for ethics-based and 'R' for resourceful. The ethics-based component ensures that the team's objectives align with collective values, promoting integrity and responsibility, in line with the ethical leadership theory (Brown, Treviño, & Harrison, 2005). The resourceful aspect requires leveraging the unique skills and resources of each team member, resonating with Drucker's (1999) concept of knowledge worker productivity. This extension is crucial in preparing students to meet the professional world's challenges, emphasizing ethical decision-making and effective resource utilization.

   The course also addresses the challenges newer generations face regarding focus and concentration. A study by Bunce, Flens, and Neiles (2010) indicates that the attention span of younger generations is being tested in a fast-paced, digital world. Therefore, the course's design caters to their unique learning needs and styles. By engaging students in setting SMARTER goals, the course not only provides a structured approach to project management but also aids in developing skills to maintain focus and manage distractions effectively. The course's comprehensive methodology contributes to the development of well-rounded individuals, ready to navigate the professional world's challenges with integrity and skill.

Upon completing the course, most students reported a significant shift in their awareness and perspective. They acknowledged their prior lack of understanding about the depth of ecological and social problems within their communities, and how this experience has changed their worldview, enhancing their societal and environmental consciousness. This transformation highlights the course's impact beyond academic learning, fostering a deeper societal awareness among students. The projects, addressing a range of local and broader societal issues, enable students to apply theoretical knowledge to real-life scenarios, deepening their understanding of change management.

The course is dynamically structured, evolving annually based on feedback and effectiveness. This ensures its relevance and responsiveness to educational needs. The structured approach to project management and focus on skill development positions the course as a key influence in shaping well-rounded individuals ready to face professional challenges with integrity and competence.

5. Conclusion

Nowadays students are expected to become lifelong learners who can work in society and global labor market that are always in flux (Demirel, 2009). Offering a transformative educational experience, the course at the University of Zagreb integrates service learning with change management education, exemplifying practical application. It stands out by bridging the gap between academic learning and real-world practice through community-based projects. The program's innovative features, including mentorship and strategic management of team dynamics, address common educational challenges like the free-rider effect, promoting individual accountability and proactive problem-solving. Students gain not only academic knowledge but also develop vital skills such as leadership, teamwork, and problem-solving, enhanced through active participation in community projects and interactions with diverse mentors.

Aligned with the university's mission, the course emphasizes civic responsibility and community engagement, preparing students to be agents of change. Service learning has been regarded as a pedagogical tool which provides students with opportunities to participate in a service activity to meet social needs and simultaneously gain benefits for themselves (Truong, Biu & Truong, 2020). By implementing Dewey and Kolb's experiential learning theories, the course transcends traditional knowledge acquisition, fostering critical thinking and application of knowledge in various contexts. Its structure and philosophy make it a successful model for incorporating service learning in higher education, enhancing academic experiences and equipping students to make meaningful societal contributions.

Educators are encouraged to adopt similar approaches, incorporating service learning and real-world applications into curricula to enhance students' understanding of complex topics and develop crucial soft skills. The integration of mentorship programs offers additional learning benefits, connecting students with industry and community insights. This approach not only prepares students as lifelong learners but also as proactive contributors to a dynamic global environment, fostering a culture of accountability and collaborative problem-solving.

References

Aggarwal, P., & O'Brien, C. L. (2008). Social loafing on group projects: Structural antecedents and effect on student satisfaction. *Journal of Marketing Education*, 30(3), 255–264. https://doi.org/10.1177/0273475308322283.

Allen, T. D., Poteet, M. L., & Burroughs, S. M. (1997). The mentor's perspective: A qualitative inquiry and future research agenda. *Journal of Vocational Behavior*, 51(1), 70–89. https://doi.org/10.1006/jvbe.1997.1596.

Allison, N. G. (2020). Students' attention in class: Patterns, perceptions of cause and a tool for measuring classroom quality of life. *Journal of Perspectives in Applied Academic Practice*, 8(2), 58–71. https://doi.org/10.14297/jpaap.v8i2.427.

Arnesson, K., & Albinsson, G. (2017). Mentorship—a pedagogical method for integration of theory and practice in higher education. *Nordic Journal of Studies in Educational Policy*, 3(3), 202–217. https://doi.org/10.1080/20020317.2017.1379346.

Bjerke, M. B., & Renger, R. (2017). Being smart about writing SMART objectives. *Evaluation and Program Planning*, 61, 125–127. https://doi.org/10.1016/j.evalprogplan.2016.12.009.

Bringle, R. G., & Hatcher, J. A. (1996). Implementing service-learning in higher education. *Journal of Higher Education*, 67, 221–239. https://doi.org/10.2307/2943981.

Brown, M. E., Treviño, L. K., & Harrison, D. A. (2005). Ethical leadership: A social learning perspective for construct development and testing. *Organizational Behavior and Human Decision Processes*, 97(2), 117–134. https://doi.org/10.1016/j.obhdp.2005.03.002.

Bunce, D. M., Flens, E. A., & Neiles, K. Y. (2010). How long can students pay attention in class? A study of student attention decline using clickers. *Journal of Chemical Education*, 87, 1438–1443. https://doi.org/10.1021/ed100409p.

Carver, R. L. (1997). Theoretical underpinnings of service learning. *Theory into Practice*, 36(3), 143–149.

Chen, Q., & Yan, Z. (2016). Does multitasking with mobile phones affect learning? A review. *Computers in Human Behavior*, 54, 34–42. https://doi.org/10.1016/j.chb.2015.07.047.

Dedehouanou, H. (2022). Strategies for implementing a "Service Learning Program" in Higher Education Institutions (HEIs): Learning strategies to improve employability. *Creative Education*, 13, 1543–1553. https://doi.org/10.4236/ce.2022.135096.

Demirel, M. (2009). Lifelong learning and schools in the twenty-first century. Procedia—*Social and Behavioral Sciences*, 1(1), 1709–1716. https://doi.org/10.1016/j.sbspro.2009.01.303.

Dewey, J. (1938). *Experience and education*. New York: Collier Books.

Doran, G. T. (1981). There's a S.M.A.R.T. way to write management's goals and objectives. *Management Review*, 70, 35–36.

Drucker, P. F. (1999). Knowledge-worker productivity: The biggest challenge. *California Management Review*, 41(2), 79–94. https://doi.org/10.2307/41165987.

Eyler, J., & Giles Jr., D. E. (1999). *Where's the learning in service-learning?* San Francisco, CA: Jossey-Bass.

Foster, H., Ooms, A., & Marks-Maran, D. J. (2015). Nursing students' expectations and experiences of mentorship. *Nurse Education Today*, 35 (1), 18–24. https://doi.org/10.1016/j.nedt.2014.04.019.

Furco, A. (1996). Service-learning: A balanced approach to experiential education. *Expanding Boundaries: Serving and Learning*, 1, 1–6.

Healey, M., & Jenkins, A. (2000). Kolb's experiential learning theory and its application in geography in higher education. *Journal of Geography*, 99(5), 185–195. https://doi.org/10.1080/00221340008978967.

Hudson, P. (2013). Mentoring pre-service teachers on school students' differentiated learning. International Journal of Evidence Based Coaching and Mentoring, 11(1), 112–128.

Jacoby, B. C. (2015). Enhancing commuter student success: What's theory got to do with it?. *New Directions for Student Services*, 2015, 3–12. https://doi.org/10.1002/ss.20122.

Kerr, N. L., & Bruun, S. E. (1983). Dispensability of member effort and group motivation losses: Free-rider effects. *Journal of Personality and Social Psychology*, 44(1), 78–94. https://doi.org/10.1037/0022-3514.44.1.78.

Jones, S. R. (2001). Where's the learning in service-learning? *The Journal of Higher Education*, 72(2), 256–258. https://doi.org/10.1080/00221546.2001.11778884.

Kirschner, P. A., & Karpinski, A. C. (2010). Facebook and academic performance. *Computers in Human Behavior*, 26(6), 1237–1245. https://doi.org/10.1016/j.chb.2010.03.024.

Kolb, D. A. (1984). *Experiential learning: Experience as the source of learning and development.* Englewood Cliffs, NJ: Prentice-Hall.

Maddux, H. C., & Donnett, D. (2015). John Dewey's pragmatism: Implications for reflection in service-learning. *Michigan Journal of Community Service-Learning,* 21, 64–73.

Mason, M. R., & Dunens, E. (2019). Service-learning as a practical introduction to undergraduate public health: Benefits for student outcomes and accreditation. *Frontiers in Public Health*, 7, 1–8. https://doi.org/10.3389/fpubh.2019.00063.

Morton, K., & Troppe, M. (1996). From the margin to the mainstream: Campus compact's project on integrating service with academic study. *Journal of Business Ethics*, 15(1), 21–32.

Nuis, W., Segers, M., & Beausaert, S. (2023). Conceptualizing mentoring in higher education: A systematic literature review. *Educational Research Review*, 41, 100565. https://doi.org/10.1016/j.edurev.2023.100565.

Omar, M. K., Khambari, M. N. M., Ma'arof, A. M., & Razali, A. B. (2022). Impact of service-learning on students employability skills: A balanced approach to empower meaningful learning experience. *Open Journal of Social Sciences*, 10, 343–364.https://doi.org/10.4236/jss.2022.102025.

Ragins, B. R., & Kram, K. E. (2007). *The handbook of mentoring at work: Theory, research, and practice*, 1st ed. Los Angeles, CA: SAGE Publications.

Resch, K., & Schrittesser, I. (2023). Using the service-learning approach to bridge the gap between theory and practice in teacher education. *International Journal of Inclusive Education*, 27(10), 1118–1132. https://doi.org/10.1080/13603116.2021.1882053.

Rosen, L. D., Carrier, L. M., & Cheever, N. A. (2013). Facebook and texting made me do it: Media-induced task-switching while studying. *Computers in Human Behavior*, 29(3), 948–958. https://doi.org/10.1016/j.chb.2012.12.001.

Santora, K. A., Mason, E. J., & Sheahan, T.C. (2013). A model for progressive mentoring in science and engineering education and research. *Innovative Higher Education*, 38 (5), 427–440. https://doi.org/10.1007/s10755-013-9255-2.

Sarabipour, S., Hainer, S. J., Arslan, F. N., de Winde, C. M., Furlong, E., Bielczyk, N., Jadavji, N. M., Shah, A. P., & Davla, S. (2022). Building and sustaining mentor interactions as a mentee. *The FEBS Journal*, 289(6), 1374–1384. https://doi.org/10.1111/febs.15823.

Schön, D. A. (1992). *The reflective practitioner: How professionals think in action*. New York, NY: Basic Books. https://doi.org/10.4324/9781315237473.

Simsek, M. R. (2020). The impact of service-learning on EFL teacher candidates' academic and personal development. *European Journal of Educational Research,* 9(1), 1–17. https://doi.org/10.12973/eu-jer.9.1.1.

Stanton, T. K., Giles, D. E. Jr., & Cruz, N. I. (1999). *Service-learning: A movement's pioneers reflect on its origins, practice, and future.* San Francisco: Jossey-Bass Publishers.

Truong, V., Biu, H., & Truong, L. (2020). Integrating community service learning into university curriculum: Perspectives from EFL teachers and students. *Language Related Researc*h, 11, 201–226. https://doi.org/10.29252/LRR.11.5.201.

Zimmerman, B. J. (2002). Becoming a self-regulated learner: An overview. *Theory into Practice*, 41(2), 64–70. https://doi.org/10.1207/s15430421tip4102_2.

Sandra Cvetko, Anica Hunjet, and Dijana Vuković

The Way to Acquire Entrepreneurial Skills through Formal Education

1. Introduction

Education is the basis of development, the success of society, and the knowledge economy. The most valuable assets are knowledge and innovation. Quality education is the basis of the success of society as a whole. Entrepreneurship can be said to have existed as long as human society has existed, and interest in entrepreneurship stems from the knowledge that the history of civilization is in a certain way a product of entrepreneurship. Today, entrepreneurship represents one of the main political, economic, and general social topics, stimulates the development of economies around the world, and generates new employment. An organization is a conscious association of people whose goal is to use the appropriate means to complete certain tasks with the least possible effort in any field. The success of organizations therefore largely depends on employees and their competencies, as well as professional development and training. According to Keeley (2009: 16) "in developed economies, the value of knowledge and information in all its forms is becoming more pronounced, and this trend has enabled the rapid spread of very fast information technology, and because of this, brains, not muscles, are at an increasingly high price, thereby widening the gap between those who are highly educated and those who are not. Countries with a high level of education very often become richer, so there is more money that can be spent on further expansion of education". Competences are sets of learning outcomes, i.e., knowledge and skills aimed at the independence and responsibility of employees. The difference between a good and a successful organization depends on the level of competence of the people employed in it, and the task of the organization is to provide employees with lifelong learning through seminars, whether formal or informal.

2. The Role and Significance of Entrepreneurship in Modern Society

The role of entrepreneurship is increasingly recognized because it stimulates economic development, reduces unemployment, and suppresses poverty. The advantages of entrepreneurship, the necessary entrepreneurial competencies and their development, and entrepreneurship education are being discussed more and more often. Educational programs in the field of entrepreneurship should increase the entrepreneurial potential of individuals through the development of entrepreneurial knowledge and skills. The outcomes of such programs should increase the number of new entrepreneurial ventures and strengthen entrepreneurial behavior. Education and training for entrepreneurship, according to Luketić (2021: 257) rests on the idea of systematically teaching a range of skills and thus developing a wide range of personality traits and professional qualities related to entrepreneurship and the entrepreneurial way of thinking and acting. According to Singer et al. (2003: 10), entrepreneurship is the result of the activities of people with a first and last name, regardless of whether they are at the head of the government, ministry, university, school, kindergarten, hospital, city, banks, or those who intend to start a business venture, those who have done so, or those who want their business to grow. At the same time, it is important to know if we are successful enough in this or if we are lagging behind others". "Entrepreneurship and entrepreneurship are best learned through personal experience but also by learning from a model. In addition, social support is important, both from schools and families as well as from society as a whole. Those pupils/students who develop entrepreneurial self-efficacy become entrepreneurs" (Miljković Krečar, 2010: 417).

Further to the above, one of the key goals of the European Commission is the promotion of entrepreneurship education at all levels, from primary school to university. It is important to develop and acquire skills, attitudes, and knowledge related to entrepreneurship and entrepreneurial culture from an early age (Huđek & Širec, 2019: 54). It is important to note that in countries, such as Croatia, with average and lower incomes, companies are mostly created "out of necessity", that is, in countries with higher incomes, entrepreneurship is enhanced by opportunities. As stated by Perić et al. (2020: 465), "the high youth unemployment rate and the challenges and demands of the labor market have led to a discussion about the effectiveness of educational programs at all levels. In this context, the efficiency and quality of vocational education and training is very important. Most students, after finishing vocational school, will not continue higher education but will find themselves on the labor market. Because of the above, vocational education should be focused on the development of skills that will meet the needs of the labor market and thus enable easier and faster employment". Oberman et al. (2013: 8) state that "entrepreneurial education has a significant role in creating the capacity of universities and individuals to cope with the complexity and uncertainty of the environment in which they operate and that it develops proactivity, innovation, individual responsibility, and readiness to take risks in making decisions and solving problems. Entrepreneurial education requires the connection of different scientific disciplines and develops the skills of a multidisciplinary approach to problem analysis and the search for solutions". Agreed guidelines and standards make a school successful, and schools that include parents, the local community, and external partners in school management have a huge impact on standards, while the rapid development of science and technology, the development of production, new production, and social relations today require entrepreneurship education" (Posavec, 2011: 226).

3. Competences, Skills, Knowledge

One of the most important priorities of the company should be the creation of entrepreneurial thinking through education and the promotion of entrepreneurship. Entrepreneurial education is key to fostering entrepreneurship. Entrepreneurial competence, according to Kőnig Sedlan (2011: 2) not only affects the development of an entrepreneurial way of thinking and more efficient use of creative potential and existing knowledge and skills, but also encourages the growth of new companies. The countries of the European Union, as well as the candidate countries for membership, have defined the development of the entrepreneurial competence of their citizens as a priority. In its document European Key Competence Framework, the European Commission included innovation and entrepreneurship among the key competencies that should be developed at all levels of education. . For this reason, the higher education system focused on entrepreneurship education is recognized as a tool for solving current economic problems (Biondić et al., 2013: 111). Entrepreneurial competence consists of certain knowledge, skills, and attitudes that are appropriate for a certain context (economic, cultural, sports, etc.). Developing entrepreneurial competence means increasing employment opportunities for young people. The research showed that students believe that there is a greater chance of getting a job for people with acquired entrepreneurial competencies. The largest part of respondents, namely 31.67 %, believe that the development of entrepreneurial competences increases the possibility of employment for young people and gave the highest score of 5, 30.00 % of respondents gave a score of 4, and 4.17 % of respondents gave a score of 1. 3.33 % of respondents are unsure and did not express their opinion. Knowledge contributes to the success of individual organizations and to the technical and scientific progress of society, while the intellectual abilities possessed by so-called intellectual workers—knowledge workers—value more than physical capital and natural inputs (Bečić et al., 2009: 118).

4. Research Methodology

The survey was completed by 1,106 respondents, namely undergraduate, graduate, and postgraduate professionals and university students at the University of the North. To obtain data, a structured questionnaire of twenty questions was used, nineteen of which were closed-ended and one open-ended. Based on the study of relevant literature in the subject area, a survey questionnaire was created. In the creation of the survey questionnaire, closed questions with an offered answer, an open question, and closed questions with offered measurement modalities using a five-point Likert scale were used. The first part of the questionnaire refers to the general data on the students, which is presented in Table 1. Questions 1–8 refer to socio-demographic structure and general questions. In question 9, respondents express their views on what contributes to the development of an entrepreneurial idea or spirit (three items). In order to prove the hypotheses, respondents were asked questions with a Likert scale from 1 to 5, or "I do not agree at all" or "I completely agree", questions from 10 to 15, and the same were related to the assessment of entrepreneurial competences, acquiring competences, listening to courses related to entrepreneurship, having basic knowledge about entrepreneurship, whether a lot can be learned from entrepreneurs, and whether it is necessary to introduce more courses related to entrepreneurship in all fields of study (five particles). The research is conducted in order to collect data, information, attitudes, and opinions of respondents about entrepreneurship, that is, entrepreneurs; entrepreneurial competencies; and education related to entrepreneurship and entrepreneurial competencies. The purpose of this paper is to see whether students in all areas of education have the opportunity to learn about entrepreneurship, whether entrepreneurship education should be available to a larger population of students, regardless of the choice of study, and whether it should be integrated into all areas of education. This research was started with this idea, which is summarized in the form of hypotheses and goals and defined in the following title. The main goal of this research is to review the situation to see if entrepreneurship education is desirable for all students, regardless of the field of study or activity. The following hypotheses are defined in the paper:

Hypothesis H1: The educational system influences the development and acquisition of entrepreneurial skills, knowledge, and attitudes and ultimately influences entrepreneurial activity and intention.

Hypothesis H2: Entrepreneurship education is essential for improving competencies and opening one's own company.

Table 1: Sociodemographic structure (N = 1106) of respondents

Questions	%	N
1. Sex		
M	40.30 %	446
F	59.70 %	660
2. Age		
18–26	73.40 %	812
27–35	13.90 %	154
36–44	8.90 %	98
45–53	3.30 %	36
54–65	0.50 %	6
3. Level of Studies		
undergraduate	68.00 %	752
graduate degree	28.00 %	306
postgraduate	4.30 %	48
4. Type of Studies		
professional	58.40 %	646
university	41.60 %	460
5. Study Program		
Electrical engineering (undergraduate)	3.26 %	36
Multimedia, design and application (undergraduate)	8.95 %	99
Production engineering (undergraduate)	4.97 %	55
Logistics and Mobility (undergraduate)	4.07 %	45
Civil engineering (undergraduate)	5.06 %	56
Civil engineering (undergraduate)	2.98 %	33
Computing and Informatics (undergraduate)	0.90 %	10
Geodesy and geomatics (undergraduate)	1.54 %	17
Nursing (undergraduate)	8.86 %	98
Physiotherapy (undergraduate)	10.67 %	118
Business and Management (undergraduate)	4.61 %	51
Food technology (undergraduate)	3.98 %	44
Communication, media and journalism (undergraduate)	4.52 %	50
Media design (undergraduate)	3.07 %	34
Music and media (undergraduate)	0.54 %	6
Multimedia (graduate)	2.71 %	30
Mechanical Engineering (graduate)	3.98 %	44
Civil engineering (graduate)	3.26 %	36

(*continued on next page*)

Table 1: Continued

Questions	%	N
Packaging, recycling and environmental protection (graduate)	1.36 %	15
Sustainable mobility and logistics management (graduate)	2.98 %	33
Nursing—management in nursing (graduate)	4.07 %	45
Communication, media and journalism (graduate)	1.09 %	12
Public relations (graduate)	2.26 %	25
Media design (graduate)	1.27 %	14
Media design (graduate)	4.70 %	52
Entrepreneurship and EU funds (postgraduate)	2.17 %	24
Media and Communication (postgraduate)	2.17 %	24
6. Study Status		
regularly	49.10 %	543
extraordinary	50.90 %	563
7. How Do You Finance Your Studies		
I am a full-time student with a subsidy from the Ministry of Education and Culture	37.30 %	413
I pay for my studies myself	58.00 %	641
my studies are fully financed by my employer	3.30 %	36
my studies are partially financed by my employer	1.40 %	16
8. You Are Employed At		
indefinite	46.50 %	514
determined	6.70 %	74
through the student service	46.80 %	518

Source: Author's work

The sample consisted of subjects (men: 40.30 % and women: 59.70 %) of younger age (18–26 years, 73.40 %) and more mature age (27–65 years, 26.60 %). selected by a deliberate random sample at the University of the North, who have regular and part-time student status (49.10 % full-time and 50.90 % part-time), undergraduate (68 %), graduate (27.70 %), and postgraduate (4.30 %) levels of study at professional (58.40 %) and university studies (41.60 %). The majority of respondents from the undergraduate study of physiotherapy (10.67 %), from the undergraduate study of multimedia, design, and application (8.95 %), and from the undergraduate study of nursing (8.86 %) took the survey. A large percentage of respondents, 58 % of them, pay for their studies, and 46.50 % of respondents work on a fixed-term basis, or 46.80 % of respondents work through the student service. In the future, the same research should be conducted at other universities in Croatia in order to get a complete picture of the entrepreneurial competencies that students acquire during their education at higher education institutions. This sample and research were carried out in the area of the University of the North, and the results obtained are suitable for obtaining indicative results and making general conclusions about entrepreneurial competences, about the knowledge and skills acquired during the study, and they can serve as a basis for further research about the role of education in entrepreneurship, their attitudes about one's own knowledge and skills, and thoughts about starting one's own entrepreneurship, but one cannot make a comparison with other universities in the Republic of Croatia, which represents a challenge in terms of research. The description of the sample is shown in Table No. 1. Among the offered answers, students chose the following: gender, age, level of study, type of study, study they are studying at, study status, method of financing studies, and method of employment (Table 1).

The first step in the analysis of the initial set of claims is the assessment of the reliability of the analyzed measurement scales (Table 2). The following table shows the Cronbach alpha coefficients for individual measuring scales (Table No. 2). Cronbach's alpha coefficient is a measure of the internal consistency of a set of statements and can take a value between 0 and 1; the closer to 1, the more reliable the measurement scale. For example, Kline (1998) states the following reliability criteria for measuring scales: if the reliability coefficient (including the Cronbach alpha coefficient) takes a value of around 0.9, the reliability can be considered excellent; if it takes a value of around 0.8, the reliability can be considered very good; and if it takes a value of around 0.7, the reliability can be considered acceptable. A reliability coefficient of less than 0.5 indicates that more than half of the observed variance could be due to random error. Measurement scales with such a low reliability coefficient cannot be considered reliable and should not be used in further analysis (Kline, 1998). Nunnally and Bernstein (1994) state that values of the Cronbach alpha coefficient already around 0.7 can be considered acceptable.

Table 2: Cronbach alpha

Case Processing Summary			
		N	%
Cases	Valid	1,106	100.0
	Excluded[a]	0	0.0
	Total	1,106	100.0

a. Listwise deletion based on all variables in the procedure.

Reliability Statistics	
Cronbach's Alpha	N of Items
0.901	29

Source: Author's work

The Cronbach Alpha coefficient 0.901 is a measure of the internal consistency of a set of statements about the development of entrepreneurship competencies, developing entrepreneurship competencies increases the opportunity for self-employment, acquiring entrepreneurship competencies contributes to success in the future job, people who attended the course during higher education have a better chance for personal success related to entrepreneurship, having basic knowledge about entrepreneurship is important and useful, one can learn a lot from entrepreneurs, it is necessary to offer more elective courses in entrepreneurship in all fields of study. The Cronbach Alpha coefficient indicates that the internal consistency with a coefficient of 0.901 is excellent. Based on the Cronbach Alpha coefficient shown in "Table 11", it can be concluded that the applied measurement scales have an excellent level of reliability or that they are valid instruments for measuring the attitudes and opinions of the respondents of the University of the North about education, entrepreneurship, competences, skills and attitudes. Table 3 shows the particle codes that were used as abbreviations for proving the hypotheses.

Table 4 shows the results of the mean values; that is, the ANOVA test compares the explained variance (caused by the input fields) with the unexplained variance (caused by the source of error). According to the presentation of the results of the ANOVA test shown in Table 4, the hypothesis can be confirmed.

Table 3: Particles with which we tested H1

AB	I believe that acquiring entrepreneurial skills will contribute to my success in my future job
AC	people who attended a course related to entrepreneurship during their higher education have a greater chance of personal success
AD	having basic knowledge about entrepreneurship is important and useful
DA	innovation (creating new products)
DB	tendency to take risks
DC	self-confidence (belief in oneself and one's abilities)
DD	workaholicism (high level of work habits)
DF	responsibility
DJ	achievement oriented
EA	acquisition of theoretical knowledge
EB	acquisition of practical knowledge
EC	acquiring knowledge through the entire education

Source: Author's work

Table 4: ANOVA test on adopted competences and their importance on success in business

Bayesian Estimates of Coefficients[a,b,c,d]					
Parameter	Posterior			95 % Credible Interval	
	Mode	Mean	Variance	Lower Bound	Upper Bound
AC = 1	3,452	3,452	0.008	3,281	3,623
AC = 2	3,598	3,598	0.004	3,468	3,728
AC = 3	4,001	4,001	0.001	3,929	4,072
AC = 4	4,098	4,098	0.002	4,017	4,179
AC = 5	4,688	4,688	0.006	4,543	4,834

a. Dependent Variable: AB
b. Model: AC
c. Regression Weight Variable: AD
d. Assume standard reference priors.

Bayesian Estimates of Error Variance[a]					
Parameter	Posterior			95 % Credible Interval	
	Mode	Mean	Variance	Lower Bound	Upper Bound
Error variance	2,374	2,383	0.010	2,192	2,590

a. Assume standard reference priors.
Source: Author's work

With an ANOVA with a margin of error of 0.5 and 95 % significance, the variance is 0.010. The variance of 0.010 indicates that the acquisition of entrepreneurial competencies contributes to success in a future job, that a greater number of courses related to entrepreneurship are necessary, and that students consider the entrepreneurial knowledge they acquire through education to be important and useful. Having basic knowledge about entrepreneurship is important and useful because students gain confidence and motivation to become proactive and creative and learn to work in a team. By adopting entrepreneurial competencies, respondents become more capable of setting and achieving goals, become more enterprising, innovative, and creative, and acquire the ability to solve problems.

Table 5: ANOVA test on the most significant competencies and their connection to success in business (innovativeness—tendency to take risks and development of self-confidence)

Bayesian Estimates of Coefficients[a,b,c,d]					
Parameter	**Posterior**			**95 % Credible Interval**	
	Mode	**Mean**	**Variance**	**Lower Bound**	**Upper Bound**
DB = 1	2,421	2,421	0.027	2,100	2,741
DB = 2	2,891	2,891	0.006	2,740	3,041
DB = 3	3,299	3,299	0.002	3,203	3,395
DB = 4	3,698	3,698	0.002	3,612	3,784
DB = 5	4,163	4,163	0.004	4,037	4,288

a. Dependent Variable: DA
b. Model: DB
c. Regression Weight Variable: DC
d. Assume standard reference priors.

Bayesian Estimates of Error Variance[a]					
Parameter	**Posterior**			**95 % Credible Interval**	
	Mode	**Mean**	**Variance**	**Lower Bound**	**Upper Bound**
Error variance	2,857	2,867	0.015	2,637	3,117

a. Assume standard reference priors.
Source: Author's work

Using ANOVA with a margin of error of 0.5 and 95 % significance, the variance is 0.015. Among the tested particles, the largest variance of 0.027 is on the DB particle, which tells us about the propensity to take risks and means that students do not have a propensity to take risks and that they should be offered a greater number of entrepreneurial courses in order to gain better knowledge and thus strengthen the competence related to the propensity to take risks. By acquiring knowledge, they will have the "courage" to take risks, and their own potential, i.e., competence, will increase, and they will be able to turn ideas into actions.

Entrepreneurial competencies are necessary in entrepreneurial education because they are the ones that give a company a competitive advantage. Limitations in the research are that the research was conducted only at the University of the North, and it would be desirable for the research to be conducted by other universities in order to be able to compare the results and derive guidelines for the development of further education for entrepreneurship in higher education. The limitation of the research also refers to the fact that it has not been established which of the respondents comes from an entrepreneurial family. This work and the conducted research have several key implications for making decisions about how to acquire knowledge, skills, and traits that are necessary for entrepreneurship. The entire research and the results presented in the research results chapter emphasize the importance of entrepreneurship education through formal education. Entrepreneurship is no longer knowledge that is traditionally passed down from generation to generation, but the necessity and duty of the entire educational system, which has the task and function of teaching entrepreneurial knowledge and tools that develop entrepreneurship and an entrepreneurial mindset. Education at higher education institutions should aim at training young people to navigate in an unsafe and complex environment. Through education, they should learn to define problems and how to come up with solutions by creating new ideas and how to communicate with the environment. Examining the thoughts and attitudes of students, the role of entrepreneurship education was explained, which will be able to solve problems faced by development through formal education of creativity, exchange of ideas, identification of problems characteristic of entrepreneurship, and taking risks. The results of a survey conducted at the University of the North show a growing interest in entrepreneurship education with the development of personal responsibility, and further research should be based on the development of awareness of a positive attitude towards entrepreneurship and the acquisition of knowledge, skills, and competencies for the future. Furthermore, further research should focus on several dimensions in order to obtain a complete picture of entrepreneurship education through formal education:

- the perception of professors of higher education institutions about the activities that are undertaken in individual courses in order to achieve skills and competences;

- the perception of professors of higher education institutions about the methods that encourage the development of entrepreneurship competencies among students;
- professor's assessment of the competences adopted by students through formal education.

The greatest contribution of this paper is the established connection between entrepreneurial education and acquired competencies necessary for work and life in the knowledge society. In the application sense, it can be concluded from the responses of the respondents (students) that there is a need for a greater number of entrepreneurial courses for entrepreneurship in formal education, which implies the creation of concepts and teaching programs according to the needs of the market and the demands of students. The obtained results, considering the number of respondents, represent the possibility of comparison with future research conducted with other higher education institutions in the Republic of Croatia.

5. Conclusion

In today's rapidly changing society, learning and knowledge have become valuable, and educational institutions should respond to the needs of the community and the economy through programs that encourage the creation of knowledge and skills related to the development of entrepreneurial competences, as this creates the basis for sustainable economic development. Entrepreneurship education should be part of compulsory education in all fields of science with the aim of acquiring entrepreneurial competencies and creating positive attitudes towards entrepreneurship inside and outside the education system. More elective courses should be offered that will enable students to acquire and upgrade the necessary entrepreneurial competencies, regardless of whether they will be entrepreneurs or entrepreneurial employees in the future, because entrepreneurial education does not only include entrepreneurs but also nurses, doctors, electrical technicians, machinists, artists, scientists, bankers, and many others.. This work wanted to raise the awareness of young people about the importance of learning for entrepreneurship, regardless of the field of science in which they upgrade or improve, because it is really one of the key links, that is, the driver of the development of innovations, which certainly results in the success of the entire economy. In addition, the conclusion of the research shows the need for the highest possible quality training of professors and teaching staff for teaching entrepreneurship competencies. The development of society, and therefore the development of higher education institutions, is based on the concepts of lifelong education and a learning society.

References

Bečić, E. et al. (2009). Međunarodne organizacije o obrazovanju odraslih. Zagreb: 1. *Agencija za strukovno obrazovanje*, 1. dio.

Biondić, I., Katavić, I., i Zelić, A. (2013). Doprinos suvremenog poduzetničkog obrazovanja povećanju zapošljivosti u Republici Hrvatskoj—studija slučaja Veleučilišta Vern. *Učenje za poduzetništvo*, 3(1), str. 111–120. https://hrcak.srce.hr/130301. Accessed on January 8, 2024.

CEPOR—centar za politiku razvoja malih i srednjih poduzeća i poduzetništva, Singer, S., Pfeifer, S., Borozan, Đ., Šarlija, N., & Oberman, S. (2003). Što Hrvatsku čini (ne)poduzetničkom zemljom—rezultati GEM 2002 za Hrvatsku. CEPOR, Zagreb. http://www.cepor.hr/GEM-brosura-2002-2011.pdf. Accessed on January 5, 2024.

Huđek, I., i Širec, K. (2019). RAZVOJ PODUZETNIČKOG POTENCIJALA KROZ OBRAZOVANJE ZA PODUZETNIŠTVO U EU. *Ekonomska misao i praksa*, (1), str. 53–78. https://hrcak.srce.hr/221025. Accessed on January 4, 2024.

Keeley, B. (2009): *Ljudski Kapital*, Educa, Zagreb.

Kline, R. B. (1998). *Principles and practice of structural equation modeling.* New York, NY: The Guilford Press.

Kőnig Sedlan, Lj. (2011). Poduzetnička kompetencija kao izvor konkurentnosti studenata na tržištu rada. Sveučilište J.J. Strossmayera u Osijeku, Ekonomski fakultet. Osijek,. Str. 2. Dostupno na URL: http://bib.irb.hr/datoteka/713484.final_EV_pod._kompetencija_i_konkurentnost_studenata.pdf. Accessed on January 6, 2024.

Luketić, D. (2021). Odgoj i obrazovanje za poduzetništvo u obveznom obrazovanju: lekcije koje učimo temeljem recentnih istraživanja. *Acta Iadertina*, 18(2), str. 255–284. https://doi.org/10.15291/ai.3607. Accessed on January 2, 2024.

Miljković Krečar, I. (2010). Razvoj poduzetničkih kompetencija u sustavu cjeloživotnog obrazovanja. *Napredak*, 151(3–4), str. 417–432. https://hrcak.srce.hr/82718. Accessed on January 2, 2024.

Nunnally, J. C., & Bernstein, I. H. (1994). The assessment of reliability. *Psychometric Theory*, 3, 248–292.

Oberman Peterka, S., Singer, S., & Alpeza, M. (2013). Poduzetničko obrazovanje: nedostajuća komponenta u stvaranju multidisciplinarnog integriranog sveučilišta. U: Čavrak, V., Gelo, T., (ur.), *Zbornik radova znanstvene konferencije Ekonomsko obrazovanje u Republici Hrvatskoj: jučer, danas, sutra* (pp. 279–301). Zagreb: Ekonomski fakultet. https://www.efzg.unizg.hr/UserDocsImages/KID/Zbornik%20radova%20Ekonomsko%20obrazovanje%20u%20RH.pdf. Accessed on January 5, 2024.

Perić, J., Oberman Peterka, S., i Getoš, Ž. (2020). ULOGA SREDNJEG STRUKOVNOG OBRAZOVANJA U RAZVOJU PODUZETNIČKIH KOMPETENCIJA UČENIKA. *Ekonomski pregled*, 71(5), str. 463–492. https://doi.org/10.32910/ep.71.5.2. Accessed on January 4, 2024.

Posavec, M. (2011). Odgoj za poduzetništvo u primarnom obrazovanju. *Učenje za poduzetništvo*, 1(1), str. 225–238. https://hrcak.srce.hr/130106. Accessed on January 6, 2024

Zuzana Birknerová and Dagmara Ratnayake Kaščáková

Links between Managerial Well-Being, Emotions, and Quality of Life

1. Introduction

Well-being has been defined as the combination of feeling good and functioning well; the experience of positive emotions such as happiness and contentment as well as the development of one's potential, having some control over one's life, having a sense of purpose, and experiencing positive relationships (Huppert, 2009). It is a sustainable condition that allows the individual or population to develop and thrive. The term subjective well-being is synonymous with positive mental health. The World Health Organization (2001) defines positive mental health as "a state of well-being in which the individual realizes his or her own abilities, can cope with the normal stresses of life, can work productively and fruitfully, and is able to make a contribution to his or her community".

Well-being has been linked to success at professional, personal, and interpersonal levels, with those individuals high in well-being exhibiting greater productivity in the workplace, more effective learning, increased creativity, more prosocial behaviors, and positive relationships (Diener, 2012; Huppert, 2013; Oishi et al., 2007). Further, longitudinal data indicates that well-being in childhood goes on to predict future well-being in adulthood (Richards & Huppert, 2011).

Social well-being was defined by Keyes (1998) as "the appraisal of one's circumstance and functioning in society" (p. 122), specifying that living has a social nature and its challenges are viewed as criteria for achieving a better quality of life. As such, well-being, as derived from the social structure, is viewed by the author Keyes (1998) through a multidimensional model made up of five dimensions:

(a) Social integration is the perceived quality of an individual's relationship with their society and community. The individual feels integrated when they have something in common with the other members of their social context;
(b) Social acceptance involves the meaning the individual has constructed of their society, based on the characteristics and qualities of others. Individuals who demonstrate higher levels of social acceptance rely on others, consider that others are able to be gentle, and believe that people can be diligent;

(c) Social contribution includes the individual's assessment of their social value: their self-efficacy and perceived responsibility, including the belief that they are an important member of the society;
(d) Social actualization refers to the individual's evaluation of how the society develops and its trajectory, evolution and potential, which implies they believe that social growth, is beneficial.
(e) Social coherence implies the individual's perception of the quality, organization and functioning of the social world. Socially healthy individuals have a realistic view of the world and the desire to give meaning to life experiences.

Diener's research shows that satisfaction with subjective well-being tends to correlate higher in confrontations with objective conditions. In the 1990s, he summarized the definitions of subjective well-being into a three-component structure, kt. it consisted of overall life satisfaction, positive mood and negative mood (Džuka & Dalbert 2002). In another contribution, Diener (1984) describes these three components of well-being: positive and negative affectivity, evaluation of satisfaction in individual areas of life and global assessment of life satisfaction.

Křivohlavý (2010) states that anyone who wants to better understand the phenomenon called "well-being" and its subjective feelings that affect well-being must be familiar with these three theories: the theory of life goals, the theory of satisfaction of life needs and the theory of the biological basis of the feeling of well-being. Theory of life goals lies in the fact that a person feels good when he has something to live for, i.e. he has a good goal set for his efforts and the realization of that goal leads to satisfaction (well-being). During this, there are deviations from the planned procedure, and this usually manifests itself in the growth of negative emotions, which may not immediately mean a reduced level of positive emotions. Norman Bradburn (1969) experimentally demonstrated that the emotion rating scale does not go from positive to negative emotions, but that we have two scales for positive and negative feelings. It is proven that the greatest negative impact on subjective well-being is a discrepancy between an individual is and what he would like to be (Křivohlavý 2010). Another important influence is the current changes in the environment, as well as in the life of the given person - it is proven that negative changes (unemployment, illness, divorce ...) reduce the level of subjective well-being. But it is also proven that subjective well-being shows a certain permanent characteristic, despite bad life circumstances (Masárová & Živčicová 2012).

Subjective well-being is evaluation of life in terms of satisfaction and balance between positive and negative effect (Figure 1). Subjective well-being is an idea arises from the social sciences that represent how one evaluates his life and includes measures of life satisfaction, a lack of depression and anxiety, and positive feelings, moods and emotions. Subjective well-being is a measure of happiness conducted by asking survey respondents how they felt about their life (Gunjan & Babita, 2015).

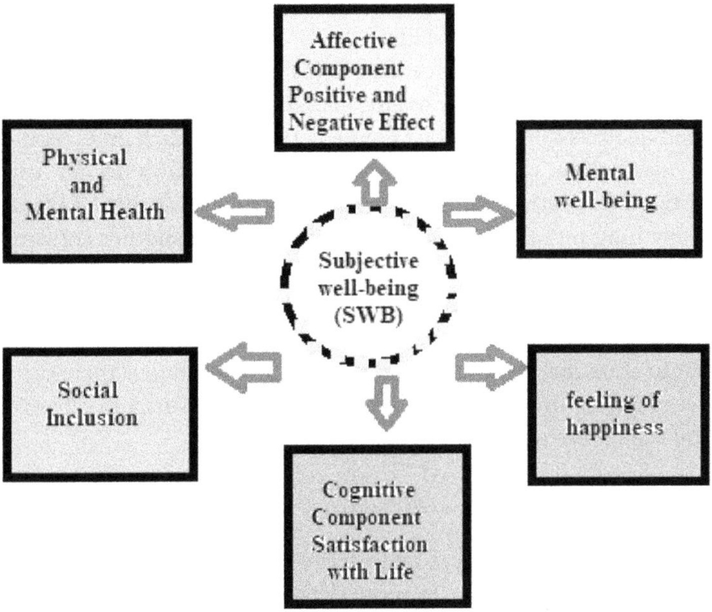

Figure 1: Main components of subjective well-being
Source: Own processing according to Sadeghi et al. (2022)

Individual subjective well-being depends on achieving satisfaction in numerous domains, including health, finance, leisure and work and given the dominant role that one´s occupation plays in modern identity. It seems quite probable that occupational factors have a significant impact on subjective well-being. Given the implications that subjective well-being, which supports productivity, life satisfaction, socially desirable behaviors and positive physical and mental health (Keyes & Waterman, 2003), can have for workplace productivity, absenteeism (Jones et al., 1991) and staff attrition, it is surprising that little attention has been given to how occupational groups can enhance the subjective well-being of workers.

Džuka (2004) devoted himself to conceptualizations of theories from various authors and finally defined four main streams of how to understand the concept of subjective well-being in connection with quality of life. The first stream sees subjective well-being and quality of life as two independent variables, between which it is not necessary to specify mutual relations. The second stream takes subjective well-being as part of quality of life. The third stream is defined by the fact that the concepts are identified. The fourth stream says that subjective well-being is an indicator of quality of life.

Well-being is probably the most frequently used equivalent of quality of life. The frequent confusion and overlapping of these two terms: subjective well-being (SWB) and quality of life—was first pointed out by a research group at the World Health Organization, which pointed out the fact that if we do not distinguish between these two terms, in that case the construct of quality of life does not provide anything more, just what is already defined in another construct, thus becoming empty. Another negative effect is the incompatibility with what is the object of the consensus of multidimensionality of the quality of life construct, which consists in the fact that multidimensionality does not refer to personal traits, but to areas that represent quality of life. The solution is therefore that the construct of quality of life does not overlap with the construct of subjective well-being and is defined by its own content (Džuka, 2014).

2. Research

The aim of the research is first of all to verify the factor structure of the Quality of Life, which we will discuss in more detail. We were also interested in the links between the variables—Quality of Life and Social Well-Being, where we wanted to find out more specifically how they are related to each other. Based on the theoretical background and the goal of the research three hypotheses are established:

- Hypothesis 1: We assume that there are statistically significant links between Quality of Life and Social Well-Being of managers.
- Hypothesis 2: We assume that there are statistically significant links between Social Well-Being and Emotions of managers.
- Hypothesis 3: We assume that there are statistically significant links between Quality of Life and Emotions of managers.

QLC12 questionnaire—For the purposes of assessing the quality of life of managers, in our research we used a modified version of the questionnaire Quality of Life—a comparative concept of the authors (Frankovský & Kovacsová, 2008), which contains twelve items, therefore we called it QLC12. Respondents expressed their level of agreement on a six-point scale: 1—strong disagreement to 6—strong agreement. In the research, we will verify the original two-factor structure, where the first factor is based on a comparison of the respondent's view of himself and society, and the second factor is based on a comparison of the quality of life in the past and the present:

F1—Me compared to others

1. Most people are doing better than me right now.
2. The quality of life in our society is higher than the quality of my life.
3. I have much less opportunities to realize my wishes than other people.
4. Society does not allow me to increase the quality of my life.
5. I cannot achieve the goals set by the society.
6. I do not manage to fulfill all my ideas.
7. Most people can afford more than I can.

F2—My past and my present

1. I assumed that I would be better off than I am now.
2. I was better off in the past than I am now.
3. I currently feel a greater lack than in the past.
4. Now I am more dissatisfied with life than in the past.
5. People's quality of life is currently lower than in the past.

Social Well-Being Questionnaire—constructed according to Keyes' study (1998) aimed at verifying the theory of well-being. The total score referred to as SocWB is obtained after reversing the items and adding up all five dimensions: Social Integration (SIn), Social Acceptance (SAc), Social Actualization (SAt), Social Coherence (SCh) and Social Contribution (SCo). The degree of agreement was indicated on a seven-point scale: 1—strongly disagree to 7—strongly agree. After reversing the poles, the statements of the SWB questionnaire with five dimensions have the following wording:

Social Integration

1. I feel I belong to something I´d call a community.
2. I feel close to other people in my community.
3. I see my community as a source of comfort.

Social Acceptance

1. People who do a favor expect nothing in return.
2. People care about other people´s problems.
3. I believe that people are kind.

Social Contribution

1. I have something valuable to give to the world.
2. My daily activities produce something worthwhile for my community.
3. I have something important to contribute to society.

Social Actualization

1. The world is becoming a better place for everyone.
2. Society has not stopped making progress.
3. Society is improving for people like me.

Social Coherence

1. The world is not too complex for me.
2. I can make sence of what is going on in the world.
3. I fint it easy to predict what will happen next in society.

Emotional Habitual Subjective Well-Being Scale or SEHP scale—this scale was introduced by Džuka and Dalbert (2002) in their research called "Elaboration and Verification of Emotional, Habitual, Subjective Well-being Scales". Using a list of descriptive words (1 almost never—2 rarely—3 occasionally—4 often—5 very often—6 almost always), participants are asked to choose how often they experience these ten emotions/states: anger, feeling of guilt, enjoyment, a shame, body freshness, fear, pain, joy, sadness and happiness.

Research sample

The total research sample consisted of 110 managers, of which 54 men (49 %) and 56 women (51 %) in the age range from 19 to 70 years with an average age of 40 years (standard deviation 12.840 years). The managers had 1–50 years of experience. The average value is 17 years of experience (standard deviation 13.069 years).

3. Results

Our output is the determination of the relationships of the variables in Table 1. We see that there are significant links between Quality of Life factors and Social Well-Being, and therefore we can write their interconnection with the equation:

$$\text{F1, F2} \uparrow \text{so} \downarrow \text{SocWB} \quad \text{at the same time} \quad \text{F1, F2} \downarrow \text{so} \uparrow \text{SocWB}$$

Table 1: Statistically significant links between social well-being and quality of life

	F1 **Me and Others**	**F2** **Past and Present**
SIn	-0.171	-0.300**
	0.073	0.001
SAc	-0.109	-0.265**
	0.258	0.005
SCo	-0.351**	-0.245**
	0.000	0.010
SAt	-0.439**	-0.328**
	0.000	0.000
SCh	-0.380**	-0.397**
	0.000	0.000
SocWB	-0.420**	-0.439**
	0.000	0.000

Source: Own processing

Based on the intensity of the links in Table 1, which we obtained by Pearson's correlation coefficient, we can also verbally interpret the following outputs.

The less managers compare themselves to their surroundings, the higher the social actualization they notice in a person. They feel that society keeps moving forward and that the world is becoming a better place for everyone. They can say that the less they compare their quality of life in the past with the present, the easier they can deal with life events and the easier it is for them to predict what will happen to their community in the near future. The opposite is true for those who constantly compare their previous quality of life with the current one, cannot understand what is happening in the world, and the whole world appears to them as a complex system. Managers who do not need to constantly compare themselves with others in their community, know very well their qualities and value for society, are aware that they contribute something valuable to their community. Managers who focus on their current quality of life and do not look behind themselves, feel closeness to people and comfort in their community. This is also true in the opposite case, when too much focus on the past is reflected in the fact that they do not feel comfortable and do not feel that they belong to any community at all. If a person has high social acceptance, believes that people are kind, care about the problems of others and in most cases are more satisfied with their quality of life.

Hypothesis 1 was *confirmed*, there are statistically significant links between Quality of Life and Social Well-Being of managers.

We continue by testing hypothesis 2. In Table 2, the first row represents the five dimensions of Social Well-Being, while the last row calculates the total Well-Being. Pearson's correlation coefficient was used to determine the links between five dimensions of Social Well-Being and ten Emotions of SEHP questionnaire.

Table 2: Statistically significant links between Social Well-Being and Emotions

	SIn	**SAc**	**SCo**	**SAt**	**SCh**	**SWB**
Anger	-0.053	-0.188*	-0.171	-0.175	-0.193*	-0.226*
	0.580	0.049	0.075	0.068	0.043	0.017
Feeling of guilt	-0.021	-0.007	-0.102	-0.117	-0.251**	-0.145
	0.831	0.942	0.287	0.224	0.008	0.132
Enjoyment	0.152	0.107	0.210*	-0.047	0.283**	0.199*
	0.113	0.268	0.027	0.627	0.003	0.037
A shame	-0.160	-0.105	-0.143	-0.087	-0.245**	-0.211*
	0.095	0.276	0.136	0.364	0.010	0.027
Body freshness	0.041	0.242*	0.221*	0.263**	0.134	0.263**
	0.668	0.011	0.020	0.006	0.162	0.006
Fear	-0.112	0.101	-0.170	0.005	-0.189*	-0.102
	0.245	0.292	0.076	0.961	0.048	0.289
Pain	0.000	-0.236*	0.034	-0.193*	-0.226*	-0.182
	0.997	0.013	0.725	0.043	0.018	0.057
Joy	0.166	0.167	-0.031	0.100	0.096	0.140
	0.082	0.081	0.747	0.299	0.320	0.144
Sadness	-0.070	-0.145	0.052	-0.159	-0.252**	-0.166
	0.470	0.130	0.592	0.097	0.008	0.083
Happiness	0.134	0.109	0.019	0.065	0.076	0.113
	0.164	0.255	0.844	0.503	0.431	0.239

Source: Own processing

We found a negative correlation between dimensions of Social Well-Being and Emotions such as anger, feeling of guilt, pain and sadness. Stronger positive correlation was found between Social Well-Being and Emotions such as enjoyment or bodily freshness. Social integration was the only one that did not show a significant connection to Emotions.

SAc ↑	if	↓ negative emotions	at the same time	↑ positive emotions
SCo ↑	if	↓ negative emotions		
SAt ↑	if	↓ negative emotions	at the same time	↑ positive emotions
SCh ↑	if	↓ negative emotions	at the same time	↑ positive emotions
SWB↑	if	↓ negative emotions	at the same time	↑ positive emotions

Hypothesis 2 was *confirmed*. There are statistically significant links between social well-being and emotions of managers.

Table 3: Statistically significant links between quality of life and emotions

	F1 **Me and Others**	**F2** **Past and Present**
Anger	0.284**	0.191*
	0.003	0.046
Feeling of guilt	0.323**	0.260**
	0.001	0.006
Enjoyment	-0.250**	-0.215*
	0.008	0.024
A shame	0.195*	0.279**
	0.042	0.003
Body freshness	-0.300**	-0.263**
	0.001	0.006
Fear	0.350**	0.202*
	0.000	0.034
Pain	0.255**	0.203*
	0.007	0.033
Joy	-0.206*	-0.214*
	0.031	0.025
Sadness	0.374**	0.247**
	0.000	0.009
Happiness	-0.146	-0.156
	0.127	0.104

Source: Own processing

Table 3 proves that there are statistically significant positive correlations between the Quality of Life factors and negative Emotions (fear, sadness), but also negative correlations between the Quality of Life factors and positive Emotions (body freshness). Happiness does not show a significant value. We write the connections between the variables as:

F1, F2↑ so ↑	negative emotions	and	F1, F2↓ so ↓	negative emotions
F1, F2↓ so ↑	positive emotions	and	F1, F2↑ so ↓	positive emotions

The more managers focus on comparing themselves with others and pay more attention to the past, not living for the present, the more they accumulate negative energy and negative feelings prevail. They do not need to constantly compare ourselves with our surroundings and compete with each other, they can live for the moment, they should leave the past behind, the more positive energy kicks in and radiates from them, the more positive emotions flow through them.

Hypothesis 3 was *confirmed*. There are statistically significant links between quality of life and emotions of managers.

4. Discussion and Conclusion

After carrying out our research, we came to two conclusions that confirmed our research hypotheses:

1. Well-being increases if the quality of life of managers increases.
2. Well-being and quality of life of managers increase if positive emotions increase and negative emotions decrease.

We found that the selected dimensions of Social Well-Being among respondents grow if they are oriented to the present and do not constantly deal with their past. Values of Well-Being also increase if the manager stop constantly comparing themselves with heir surrounding, know their qualities and are able to appreciate themselves. Such people more easily overcome obstacles in life, know how to establish contacts with people in their community, and create an environment in which they feel good. They are optimistic, believe in the kindness of people and are interested in their problems. All these findings, which tally with the literature we studied, also apply in the opposite case.

The second finding of the research was that Emotions also play a significant role in the degree of Social Well-Being and Quality of Life. The quality of a life of managers increases when, as already mentioned, their life comes first, and they live for the present. Only then they can enjoy life and experience positive emotions more often. Therefore, we agree with the statement of Křivohlavý (2013) that a more satisfied person experiences positive emotions more often and negative emotions less often. We note that by focusing on the past and comparing yourself with surroundings, a person contributes to the accumulation of bad energy inside of them. We also agree with Pendleton and Furnham (2012) that emotionally unstable people are perpetually dissatisfied. We further see a similarity with the study by Hrozenská (2008), who claims that well-being reflects a range of positive and negative reactions that satisfy the needs of the individual and are accompanied by pleasant bodily sensations. In our research, it was precisely the emotions of enjoyment and body freshness.

The recorded negative links between Well-Being and negative Emotions (anger, feeling of guilt, pain, sadness) is also in line with the opinion of Diener, Lucas and Oishimi (2002), that well-being is a broad concept of what affects the well-being of an individual, but one of these factors, in addition to life satisfaction, positive/negative emotions, the meaning and purpose of life, as well as the absence of pain. People who are more satisfied with their lives are constantly looking for new challenges and developing their knowledge. People, in this case managers are recommended to find out what they are really good at and continue to improve in it. They should set goals for the future that will lead to their satisfaction. The best thing is to look for the bright side in everything, not to be scared to leave the past behind, and walk into the day with a smile.

Acknowledgment

The compilation of this chapter was supported by the research grant project KEGA No. 018PU-4/2023.

References

Bradburn, N. M. (1969). *The structure of psychological well-being*. Chicago: Aldine.

Diener, E. (1984). Subjective well-being. *Psychological Bulletin*, 95(3), 542–575.

Diener, E., Lucas, R. E., & Oishi, S. (2002). Subjective well-being: The science of happiness and life satisfaction. In C. R. Snyder & S. J. Lopez (Eds.), *Handbook of positive psychology* (pp. 463–473). Oxford University Press.

Diener, E. (2012). New findings and future directions for subjective well-being research. *American Psychologist*, 67(8), 590–597.

Džuka, J. (2004). Kvalita života a subjektívny pohoda-teórie a modely, podobnosť a rozdiely. In J. Džuka (Ed.), *Psychologické dimenzie kvality života*. Prešov: FFPU.

Džuka, J. (2014). *Subjektívne hodnotená kvalita života—validita a rentabilita merania*. Prešov: FFPU.

Džuka, J., & Dalbert, C. (2002). Vývoj a overenie validity Škál emocionálnej habituálnej subjektívnej pohody (SEHP). *Československá psychologie*, 46, 234–250.

Frankovský, M., & Kovácsová, A. (2008). Posudzovanie kvality života nezamestnanými—komparatívny koncept. In D. Fedáková & M. Kentoš (Eds.), *Psychológia práce a organizácie 2008* (pp. 95–101). Košice: Spoločenskovedný ústav SAV.

Gunjan, S., & Babita, T. (2015). Subjective well-being for employees in an organization. *Indian Journal of Health and Wellbeing*, 6(5), 1154–1159.

Hrozenská, M. (2008). *Sociálna práca so staršími ľuďmi a jej teoreticko-praktické východiská* (1st ed.). Martin: Osveta.

Huppert, F. A. (2009). Psychological well-being: Evidence regarding its causes and consequences. *Applied Psychology: Health and Well-Being*, 1(2), 137–64. https://doi.org/10.1111/j.1758-0854.2009.01008.x.

Huppert, F. A., & So, T. T. C. (2013). Flourishing across Europe: Application of a new conceptual framework for defining well-being. *Social Indicators Research*, 110(3), 837–861.

Jones, T. M. (1991). Ethical decision making by individuals in organizations: An issue-contingent model. *The Academy of Management Review*, 16(2), 366–395. https://doi.org/10.2307/258867.

Keyes, C. L. M. (1998). Social well-being. *Social Psychology Quarterly*, 61(2), 121–140. https://doi.org/10.2307/2787065.

Keyes, C. L. M., & Waterman, M. B. (2003). Dimensions of well-being and mental health in adulthood. In M. H. Bornstein, L. Davidson, C. L. M. Keyes, & K. A. Moore (Eds.), *Well-being: Positive development across the life course* (pp. 477–497). Lawrence Erlbaum Associates Publishers. New Jersey.

Křivohlavý, J. (2010). *Pozitivní psychologie* (2nd ed.). Praha: Portál.

Křivohlavý, J. (2013). *Psychologie pocitů štěstí. Současný stav poznání.* Praha: Grada.

Masárová, T., & Živčicová, E. (2012). *Meranie kvality života* (1st ed.). Žilina. Georg.

Oishi, S., Diener, E., & Lucas, R. E. (2007). The optimum level of well-being: Can people be too happy? *Perspectives on Psychological Science*, 2(4), 346–360.

Pendleton, D., & Furnham, A. (2012). *Leadership: All you need to know.* London: Palgrave Macmillan. https://doi.org/10.1057/9780230354425.

Richards, M., & Huppert, F. A. (2011). Do positive children become positive adults? Evidence from a longitudinal birth cohort study. *Journal of Positive Psychology*, 6(1), 75–87.

Sadeghi, A. R., Ebadi, M., Shams, F., & Jangjoo, S. (2022). Human-built environment interactions: The relationship between subjective well-being and perceived neighborhood environment characteristics. *Scientific Reports*, 12(1), 21844. https://doi.org/10.1038/s41598-022-25414-9.

World Health Organization. (2001). *The world health report 2001: Mental health: New understanding, new hope*. Geneva: World Health Organization.

Kerstin Knees

The Impact of Immigration on the School Performance of Natives: A Literature Review

1. Introduction

The main interest is to clarify the question of whether there is research literature and studies in Germany or abroad that measure the influence of migrant children on non-migrant children in the classroom, as the number of children with a migrant background is increasing sharply in public schools in Germany. This raises further questions, e.g., whether the children influence each other due to language barriers, whether the classroom climate is changed positively or negatively, whether or not it is possible to realize fixed curricular goals (Esser, 2006).

The results of the education reports, in particular the last Pisa-report from 2022, are poor, the performance of pupils is falling in all subjects in all federal states. The results are particularly disastrous in the big cities and in urban social hotspots.

Although the federal government has significantly increased state spending on education, pupils' performance is not improving, but deteriorating. Around a fifth of pupils leave school without a qualification and without basic reading, writing and maths skills. The biggest change in the classes is the sharp increase in the number of children who have recently immigrated and often only come into contact with the German language here. The educational studies of recent years show that children with a migrant background in particular are inferior to the performance of German pupils at school. A lack of language skills causes difficulties in all subjects, which often leads to poorer results for foreign pupils.

This article examines the question whether children with a migrant background and children without a migrant background influence each other's learning (Allemann-Ghionda et al., 2010). With regard to the educational as well as from a social perspective, it is important to know more about the relationship between the proportion of immigrants in school classes, the educational performance of pupils with an immigrant background and native pupils, because the goal for a society should be to shape educational policy in such a way that both pupils with an immigrant background and native pupils can perform well, so that overall economic prosperity can be guaranteed in the long term.

2. Backround of This Study

In contemporary times, numerous Western are witnessing a surge in the enrollment of immigrant children in their educational institutions. According to Jenssen and Rasmussen (2011), this trend is attributed to three primary factors. In Firstly, there is a general increase in the immigrant population across most Western countries. Secondly, immigrants tend to concentrate in urban residential areas, particularly in large cities, thereby augmenting the proportion of immigrant children in schools located in these urban centers (Zavodny, 1999). Thirdly, in response to a high concentration of immigrant students, exacerbating the existing imbalance (Rangvid, 2010). The potential issue arising from this imbalance between native and immigrant children in schools in underscored by research highlighting the often-subpar academic performance of immigrant children compare to the native counterparts (Ammermueller, 2007; Entorf & Lauk, 2008). Despite existing literature exploring various explanations for the educational disparities among immigrant children, such as language skills, socioeconomic background, and school characteristics, there remains a notable research gap concerning the impact of attending a school substantial immigrant student population for native students. Addressing this gap is crucial for a more comprehensive understanding of the factors contributing to the academic performance of native students in Western countries (Jensen & Rasmussen, 2011). The data was obtained from research international studies over the period 2006–2023. The analysis included a total of thirty-seven papers. The aim of the literature review is to identify and summarize international empirical studies that relate to the question of the influence of migration on non-migrant children in classrooms and examine determinants of the learning context. This implies that it is predominantly research from countries that, like Germany, have a high proportion of migrants in society. Studies whose samples consist of homogeneous learning groups with a low proportion of migrants are therefore excluded. The studies analyzed here relate to the public and not the private schools in the individual countries

The literature review was carried out in the period from October 2023 to January 23, 2024. The search was carried out in the following databases: Elsevier, Google scholar, OECD.org., fachportal-paedagogik.de.

Table 1: The studies were selected according to the following criteria

Inclusion	Exclusion
Studies from different countries	No teacher interviews
Studies from different years after 2000	No school experiments
Studies with large cohorts	No comparison of public schools
State schools within the studies, across districts or within states	No expert interviews
National Studies	No Studies before PISA 2001
International PISA Study	No newspaper articles or other media other than the databases mentioned

3. Results

3.1. International Studies

Since the publication of the "Coleman Report" in the 1960s, educational sociologists have been interested in understanding why the school context, particularly the socioeconomic status (SES) and ethnic composition of the school, has an impact on academic achievement that accounts for more than individual factors. The existence of a negative correlation between the concentration of immigrant children in school classes and student achievement is a well-documented empirical conclusion in American and European educational sociology (Felouzis, 2003; Portes & Hao, 2004; Fekjær & Birkelund, 2007). However, the empirical studies that attempt to explain this regularity are far fewer in the international research literature, and there is a long list of potential causes and unexplained mediating mechanisms. Some studies examine only partial student performance, reducing the research to specific subjects, such as maths, while other studies produce contradictory or ambiguous results.

In a 2020 study, Van der Werf analyzed the effects of the wave of Indonesian immigration to the USA. This was the first wave of immigration from Indochina. More than 250,000 people were permanently settled in regions and a positive spillover effect occurred. The immigrants mainly came from families with a high level of education and with parents who were immediately employed in the USA. In addition, the American government provided funding so that these children could attend American universities. These combinations also had a positive effect on the native students, who also improved their performance, especially in post-secondary education. Overall, this speaks in favor of planned migration and the provision of financial resources to enable all students to receive a good education (Van der Werf, 2020).

A Dutch study found that pupils with a higher proportion of immigrants in primary school were more likely to attend lower levels of education and more likely to drop out of secondary school. A higher concentration of immigrants in secondary school also increases the likelihood of dropping out of school. Previous studies seem to have underestimated this effect (Haelermans & Heers, 2016).

In Italy, a study was conducted by Tonello in 2015 to identify the differences between native and non-native pupils in secondary schools. The results show that the proportion of pupils with a migrant background has a weak negative influence on the test results of native Italian pupils. An increase of 1 percentage point in the proportion of pupils with a migrant background lead to a decrease of 0.043 % in the average test results of native pupils. In maths, the research team found no differences in performance results (Tonello, 2015).

The results of Ballatore et al. show that the PEC effect is clear in their studies: if a pupil with a migrant background joins a school class and an Italian, a native-speaking pupil leaves the class, the results in a class are already reduced in language and maths, and this is even clearer if the first generation of immigrants is taken into account in the studies (Ballatore et al., 2018).

In Israel, the results are different. In 2009, a study by Gould et al. found that an increasing proportion of migrant pupils has a negative impact on the native population in many ways: the performance of native pupils deteriorates, school choice changes and the quality of school-leaving qualifications also deteriorates. In their study on the mass integration of Jews from the former Soviet Union at the beginning of the 1990s, they validated a negative impact on the passing of final examinations by native fifth graders (Gould et al., 2009).

Similar developments are emerging in Denmark. The study by Jensen, which is based on the data from the Pisa study, shows that the test results of native Danish schoolchildren fall significantly when the proportion in a school class is 50 % or more. For young people with an immigrant background, their performance results fall when the proportion of immigrants is 10 % or more. A year later, a further study concluded that the proportion of immigrants in classrooms should not exceed 50 %, as Danish pupils' performance dropped significantly above this level. This was nonetheless a call to action for politicians (Jensen, 2011). Another study by Rangvid (2007), which was carried out in Copenhagen, found that the proportion of immigrants in class groups should not exceed 40 %, as otherwise the native pupils would drastically lose their performance level. Overall, Denmark has a number of studies that all show that a high proportion of immigrants in class groups has a negative impact on the reading and maths skills of both immigrants and native pupils.

In Norway, children are assigned to schools in their neighborhood, although the state reserves the right to place pupils with very poor Norwegian language skills in other schools. The state distribution means that refugee children and children with a migrant background are distributed throughout the country and are not just concentrated in urban centers, as the allocation to municipalities must be maintained for five years. In recent years, the numbers have risen sharply due to refugee movements, such as those from Syria since 2015. The studies by Green and Iversen (2022) show that the maths skills of Norwegian pupils deteriorate significantly when the proportion of migrants in classes is high. This cannot be confirmed for English and Norwegian, but it is difficult to determine values in the languages, as children who do not speak Norwegian as their mother tongue usually receive separate language lessons and English lessons are mostly taught by Norwegian teachers and therefore Norwegian is also used in English lessons to explain content. The majority of refugees and migrants in Norway come from Africa, the Middle East, former Yugoslavia and Asia (97 %). According to Green and Iversen, it is mainly the first three areas of origin mentioned that have a negative effect on the native pupils, with African pupils and pupils from the Middle East in particular having a negative impact on the performance of Norwegian pupils in maths. This was particularly evident in studies of siblings who go to the same school but study in different classes. In classes where the proportion of immigrants was very high, the results were significantly worse than in neighboring classes with a lower proportion. Among children with a migrant background, it was also noticeable that children who grew up socially disadvantaged and uneducated by their parents in their home country performed very poorly and found it particularly difficult to catch up in Norway (Green &Iversen, 2020).

3.2. Studies in Germany

The majority of research on this topic took place in the first ten years after the turn of the millennium (2001–2010); there are few more recent studies.

Whether pupils with a migrant background influence pupils without a migrant background in their school performance has hardly been investigated to date, but rather the question of how the proportion of migrants in schools or classes affects the performance of migrants. Stanat wrote in 2006 that she does not see any influence, but rather the difficult social background as an aggravating factor in the pupils' educational path. In 2008, Stanat and Walter posed the question of whether the homogeneity of migrant groups in the classroom has an effect on the academic performance of these migrants. They found that there were no effects for groups of pupils from the former USSR, but there were effects for pupils of Turkish origin, but only from a proportion of 40 % in class groups. The study by Kristen (2008) in primary schools comes to the conclusion that ethnic and social reasons do not play a role in pupil composition and that the proportion of migrants does not have a negative effect on learning groups.

In the school year 2022/2023 1.6 million pupils already had a migration background. Almost every second child under the age of 10 in Germany will have a migrant background in 2022 (bpb, July 2022). The new OECD study from 2022 concludes that in almost all industrialized countries except Germany, the school performance of children with a migrant background improved with the length of their families' stay. In Germany, on the other hand, school performance deteriorated significantly.

There was a special evaluation of the 2022 PISA study in which children with a migrant background were analyzed separately. Migrant children from seventeen countries were compared with each other. According to the evaluation, Germany is one of the countries in which the differences in performance between pupils with a migrant background and those without are most pronounced. According to the study, over 25 % of first-generation pupils who were not born in Germany and whose parents come from abroad do not even reach the basic level in maths. Among young people of the second generation who were born here, the proportion is even higher than 40 % (OECD.org.).

The results for pupils in Germany 2022 are poor, the worst ever measured. The performance gap between socially disadvantaged pupils and non-disadvantaged pupils remains large in Germany; more than in other countries, social background still determines educational performance.

In addition to analyses of pupils' social environment, Pisa studies regularly analyzes disparities caused by immigration. Young people who have immigrated themselves showed lower competences in Pisa 2012 compared to Pisa 2003. Another challenge for the education system in Germany is the high level of heterogeneity and the large number of countries of origin from which the children and young people come (Stanat et al., 2010). In Pisa 2018, almost 22 % of 15-year-olds came from the former Soviet Union, Turkey and Poland. Stanat et al. reported in 2022 that over 30 % of pupils in the fourth grade, i.e., at the end of primary school, belong to the first generation and come from Arab countries. Some countries in the OECD study show lower maths skills for young people with a migrant background compared to those without. In the Netherlands and in the Czech Republic are also differences for average mathematical competence. A more differentiated look at the changes in the years 2012–2022, i.e., just ten years, shows that the mathematical competences for pupils with and without a migration background have fallen significantly in most of the countries. In 2023 many refugees now come from Arab countries such as Syria and Iraq. Particularly for first-generation pupils and young people from Turkey and Arab countries now, there is a large gap to young people without a migration background. For almost all immigrant young people, the educational qualifications of their parents are lower than those of native-born young people. It should be emphasized that since PISA 2012, significantly fewer pupils have stated that they speak German at home. Particularly in families in which both the young people and their parents were born abroad, the proportion has fallen considerably compared to PISA 2012 (www.oecd.org).

4. Discussion

The initial question of whether migrants have an influence on the performance of non-migrants in classrooms has not yet been conclusively answered. There are international studies, such as studies in Denmark, Israel and Norway, which say that there is a measurable influence on the performance of non-migrants; then there are studies which say that this influence only affects certain subjects such as maths and there are studies which say that it has no effect at all. In Europe, a high influx of migrants comes from Arab countries, Turkey, Afghanistan and African countries. They are spread all over Europe, but not to the same extent if you compare Germany with other European States. In countries such as Germany, Austria, France and the Netherlands, where there is a high influx, the high proportion of migrants has an impact on the respective societies and therefore also on the school landscape (El Mafalaani, 2020).

In Germany, as in many other countries, there are social differences in the population, so that one can speak of social inequality, these are also reflected in the education system.

The IQB study, which measures pupils' skills in German and English, shows also an enormous decline in skills in German between 2015 and 2022. The differences between young people with social disparities also increased significantly between 2015 and 2022. Parents who have little cultural capital can hardly support their children on their educational path. Parents with a high level of cultural capital have children who perform better in both, German and English. Young people with a migrant background have achieved increasingly lower standards of competence in German and English between 2009 and 2022, particularly among young people who were also born abroad (www.iqb.hu-berlin.de).

The PISA study from 2006 and the IGLU study from the same year have already shown that, particularly in Germany, children's opportunities for advancement and education are clearly dependent on their family background and the more socially disadvantaged the child grows up, the greater the social disadvantage is. As already mentioned, there are no studies, which answer the research question concrete, there are no larger cross-sectional or longitudinal studies. It is therefore not possible to measure the influence of migrant children on the educational success of non-migrant children.

5. Conclusion

After analyzing the international studies, it would be necessary for Germany to participate in the same studies. However, this has hardly taken place to date. The studies that have been carried out in Germany to date, such as the IQB study, VERA or the TiMMS study, analyzes the skills performance of German pupils and also that of pupils with a migrant background, but they do not ask about the mutual influence on the acquisition of skills.

Pupils have to work and learn with co-operative learning methods in class, that often means that the native speakers have to wait for the non-native speakers and take them into consideration, which in the medium and long term means that the learning group as a whole can learn less material. If you look at this over several school years, it becomes clear that there is an influence between the two groups of pupils, just as there is in all other countries. As Germany is one of the countries with the highest immigration flows in the world, it should be politically (educationally) desirable for the influence to be scrutinized in order to possibly bring about changes in the school system. As this has not happened so far, schools cannot adapt to the new immigration figures in schools and there is a risk that Germany's educational results will continue to fall. It should be noticeable that German studies show that student performance has deteriorated significantly since 2015 and that the increase in refugees has risen sharply since 2015 and that a connection could be sought, especially because it is known that educational results are particularly poor in federal states, cities and neighborhoods where there are high social disparities.

References

Allemann-Ghionda, C. et al. (Eds.). (2010). *Migration, Identität, Sprache und Bildungserfolg*. Weinheim. https://doi.org/10.25656/01:6942.

Ammermüller, A. (2007). Poor background or low returns? Why immigrant students in Germany perform so poorly in the programme for international student assessment. *Education Economics*, 15(2). https://doi.org/10.1080/09645290701263161.

Ballatore, R. M., Fort, M., & Ichino, A. (2018). *Tower of Babel in classroom: Immigrants and natives in Italian schools*. USA: The University of Chicago Press Journals.

Colding, B., Husted, L., & Hummelgaard, H. (2009). Educational progression of second-generation immigrants and immigrant children. *Economics of Education Review*, 28(4). https://doi.org/10.1016/j.econedurev.2007.08.004.

El-Mafaalani, A. (2020). *Mythos Bildung: die ungerechte Gesellschaft, ihr Bildungssystem und seine Zukunft*. KiWi.

Entorf, H., & Lauk, M. (2008). Peer effects, social multipliers and migrant at school: An international comparison. *Journal of Ethnic and Migration Studies*, 34(4). https://doi.org/10.1080/13691830801961639.

Esser, H. (2006). *Migration, Sprache und Integration* (AKI-Forschungsbilanz, 4). Berlin.

Fekjaer, S. N., & Birkelund, G. E. (2007/2009). Does the ethnic composition of upper secondary schools influence educational achievement and attainment? A multilevel analysis of the Norwegian case. *European Sociological Review*, 23(3), S. 309–323.

Felouzis, G. (2003). *La segregation ethnique au college et ses consequences*. Revue francaise de sociologie.

Felouzis, G., & Fouquet-Chauprade, B. (2019). *School segregation in France: The role of public policies and stakeholder strategies*.

Gould, E. D., Lacy, V., & Paserman, M. D. (2009). *Does immigration affect the long-term educational outcomes of natives?* Quasi-experimental evidence. *The Economic Journal*, 119(540). https://doi.org/10.1111/j.1468-0297.2009.02271.x.

Green, C., & Iversen, J. M. V. (2020). Refugees and the educational attainment of natives: Evidence from Norway. *Economics of Education Review*, 88. https://doi.org/10.1016/j.econedurev.2022.102258.

Green, C., & Iversen, J. M. V. (2022). The effect of class size in schools on student outcomes. In A. R. Paloyo & O. Yerokhin (Eds.), *Critical perspectives on economics of education*. Routledge. https://doi.org/10.4324/9781003100232-8.

Haelermans, C., & Heers, M. (2016). *The effects of immigrant student concentration on educational outcomes of native and immigrant students. Economics of Education Review*, 78.

Jensen, P., & Rasmussen, A. W. (2011). The effect of immigrant concentration in schools on native and immigrant children's reading and math skills. EconPapers. https://doi.org/10.1016/j.econedurev.2011.08.002.

Kristen, C. (2008). *Schulische Leistungen von Kindern aus türkischen Familien am Ende der Grundschulzeit.* Befunde aus der IGLU-Studie. *Kölner Zeitschrift für Soziologie und Sozialpsychologie, Sonderheft*, 48, S. 230–251.

Portes, A., & Hao, L. (2004). The schooling of children of immigrants: Contextual effects on the educational attainment of the second generation. PNAS. https://doi.org/10.1073/pnas.0403418101.

Rangvid, B. S. (2007). Living and learning separately? Ethnic segregation of school children in Copenhagen. *Sage Journals*, 44(7). https://doi.org/10.1080/00420980701302338.

Rangvid, B. S. (2010). School choice, universal vouchers and native flight from local schools. *European Sociological Review*, 26(3). https://doi.org/10.1093/esr/jcp024.

Stanat, P., & Walter, O. (2008). Der Zusammenhang des Migrantenanteils in Schulen mit der Lesekompetenz; Differenzierte Analysen der erweiterten Migrantenstichprobe von PISA 2003. In: *Zeitschrift für Erziehungswissenschaft.* Springer.

Stanat, P. et al. (2010). Schülerinnen und Schüler mit Migrationshintergrund. In E. Klieme, C. Artelt, N. Hartig, O. Jude, M. Köller, Prenzel et al. (Hrsg.), *PISA 2009. Bilanz nach einem Jahrzehnt* (S. 200–230). Münster: Waxmann.

Tonello, M. (2015). Peer effects on non-native students on natives'educational outcomes: Mechanisms and evidence. *Empirical Economics*, 51, 242–246.

Van der Werf, C. (2020). *The impact of refugees on native's students academic achievement.* Germany.

Zavodny, M. (1999). *Determinants of recent immigrant's locational choices.* USA: EconPapers.

Internet

www.bpb.de

www.bzga.de

www.iqb.hu-berlin.de

www.OECD.org

Martins Veide

Time Issues in the Learning Process

1. Introduction

Time is one of the most mysterious aspects of one's life. One can feel shortage of time, but at the same time experience time as limiting. In line with the post classical values and globalization, time turns out to be more important than space. A person is more defined by belonging to a particular generation rather than being defined by the place from which they come. When evaluating "what a person is like?" a greater emphasis is given to the birth date, rather than birthplace—youth is deemed to be better than elderly days. Despite the theory of psychosocial development of human beings that the experience brought by middle or late adulthood is as important as the experience obtained in youth (Erikson et al., 1994) and research that shows that people can continue to develop even in an old age and experience life as fulfilling as never before (Vaillant, 2015), can be creative and productive in a wide variety of spheres even beyond the age of eighty and ninety (Lehman, 2017), most people associate old age with regression and dullness—senility, illness, and deterioration of judgment in old age seem natural and inevitable, causing people serious concerns about their existence in time. "You always look so young!" is perceived mostly as a compliment. Many people who have negative stereotypes about age hide it from themselves by pretending that aging does not matter, denying all emotions associated with aging, desperately trying to remain young, and essentially refusing to learn from the new experiences which are offered by the next phases of life.

The verdict "new is better than old!" also is reflected with technologies, products, design, solutions, methods, research, monographs … When setting evaluation criteria novelty often becomes more important than the meaning of learning content. References are often valued higher if they include more recent publications. Passing time is gradually taking leading positions in the everyday life, including the learning process.

The question on how to curb the dictate of time and at the same time not to waste one's life on unimportant minutiae is related to the art of living or, as described by Göhlich and Zifras (2007), the learning dimension of living-learning.

The *aim* of this article is to summarize and analyze issues related to the problem of time on the basis of the existential concept.

Research method: analysis of scientific literature and sources, based on the phenomenological approach.

2. Attitude towards Death in Relation to the Idea of Limited Time

In the context of living-learning the relevance of one's attitude towards death appears. According to Heidegger (2023), real living or authentic existence is "being towards death" (*das Sein zum Tode*), that is, a person opens to being when faced with "nothing" (*das Nichts*). Yalom (2020) postulates that death is a condition that makes an authentic life possible. With that one does not mean a specific event. Real, original living is associated with an attitude towards death that is not changing dependent on someone dying nearby or not. Interpreting death as a limit that gives a meaning to life, Schmid (2021) points out to the necessity to find an attitude towards death to be able to the value of living and growing old meaningfully.

Along with the paradigm shift in Western culture at the end of the 19th century and the beginning of the 20th century, faith in an absolute and objective meaning that stands above everything else is lost. Nietzsche (2022) announces the change with the often quoted words "God is dead". These words refer not only to the decline of the authority of the church. Continuation: "we have killed him" indicates that everyone who has their apotheosis of ideals, the "right" order of things, is involved. As Heidegger (2015) argues, here one is talking about the sensual world in general, about ideals that include the purpose of life, rise above life itself and thus determine it from above and outside. Garfield (1975) concludes that the collapse of the belief system that provides traditional values, ideals and spiritual fulfillment has forced Western people to confront an existential vacuum and, in this way, has contributed to the tendency of denying death.

In a time when the religious view of life was dominant, death was seen as a "doorway" to a better, more complete existence that continues in a wonderful afterlife beyond the reach of mortals. In the modern life where belief in afterlife is eroding, people increasingly perceive death as a "wall" where the journey of life ends (Feifel, 1977). Even for those people who regularly attend church the subject of physical decay of the body is often too fearful of a subject to contemplate or talk about.

In the context of learning, the question of death seems inappropriate by many nowadays. Nevertheless, attitude towards death is closely related not only to living-learning, but also knowledge-learning, the prerequisite of which is the recognition of one's ignorance. Disinterest in death most often protects a person from confessing one's ignorance. This is especially evident when the fear of death touches those who do not think about death. The view that "it is normal to be afraid of death" does not stand up to criticism in the context of knowledge-learning because, as Socrates noted, to fear death is nothing else than to appear to be wise, without being so; for it is to appear to know what one does not know (Plato, 2023).

Despite the need to find meaning anew, denial of death creates a constant sense of not being able to do something in time and prompts a person to live in an autopilot at a stressful pace, conform to countless standards, and ultimately leaving no time for discovering the meaning of life. This paradox has been expressed by Baudrillard (2012) in this comparison: just as the need to say something becomes especially pressing when there is nothing to say, the will to live becomes especially persistent when the meaning of life has been lost.

Old age is also losing its meaning, which, thanks to the "victory of science over death", is becoming available to more and more people. As Baudrillard (2022) observes, the increase in average life expectancy has led to discrimination against old age, which logically follows the death discrimination. Elderly people are no longer the wise ones, but rather envying the young ones. At the same time, young people fear aging. With the fading of the meaning of old age, lifelong learning also loses its importance.

Despite the mass information available and its continuous increase, death for a modern-day individual remains a great enigma. Death remains a problem that cannot be resolved in a usual way—with the help of science and machine technologies. And this problem appears to be important not because every life ends with death, but because it creates a lot of anxiety for many people, which deprives satisfaction with life. Almost everyone experiences the anxiety to a greater or lesser extent about the future "wall" where the life journey will inevitably end. Still, often it is not realized and, as shown by the observations of the therapists, often is explained with other, inadequate reasons (Yalom, 2022).

Although the modern person tries to avoid the word "death" in their lexicon, there is one exception. Significantly this word is used in the context of time. In essence it indicates limited time, and often creates anxiety associated with it. It is the English word used as "due date", which is used untranslated also in other languages—*deadline*.

3. Busyness as Phenomenon of "lack of time"

Every third student considers lack of time to be limiting their quality of life. Considering own laziness, which is often described as "wasted time", almost half of all students face the time problem (Veide, 2016). When the busy teacher or student says, "I don't have time!" they do not think that what they don't have might not exist at all. With this they mean that they lack time. They believe that time exists, and that it can be *owned*. Hence, they are frustrated that they cannot control their "own" time. One feels guilt for own incompetence, attributes to oneself laziness, tries to correct the situation by learning "time management". This attitude is based on the notion that any meaningful behavior is a means to an end—as if behavior should always be instrumental. Interpreting activity as a socially recognized, goal-directed behavior, the result of which is a corresponding socially or materially beneficial change, a person seems to be living an "active life", however, twisted with fuss, and haste, and losing a deep sense of self-awareness. In fact, such activity, which Fromm (2020) calls *alienated activity* and contrasts with natural spontaneous activity, means *being busy*. And the busier an individual is, the more they distance themselves not only from other people and their experiences, but also from themselves and their own experience. It is important to note that such alienated activity is often not related to any interest in the activity itself. An individual who is *busy* with learning is not interested in the learning process itself. One must study to receive a document certifying one's education, to later obtain a certain status as an employee or employer, in order to obtain material resources. But if the goal is not reached, learning itself is not experienced as a fulfilling living. It is accompanied by escape into the future, respectively—a hope that "real life will begin after …"

Busyness can be treated as avoidance (scotomization)—a psychological defense mechanism. Busyness is an effective way to avoid and keep oneself at a comfortable distance from thoughts about life and death, from complex questions, such as: Have I chosen an appropriate career? Do I devote sufficient time for myself, family, and children? Is my life filled with meaning? Psychological defense mechanisms are responses to fear. A busy person is characterized by the fear of being "nothing", as well as the fear of facing their fears. Therefore, busyness does not only refer to external activities, but also to one's mind. Krishnamurti (2020) concludes that most of us would like to have our minds to be so busy that we would not have the opportunity to see ourselves as we really are. A constantly busy mind protects against introspection, which fatally threatens one's very habitual concepts about oneself.

Avoidance is also related to the fear of unpleasant frustrations that could arise as a result of one's spontaneous activity, if it does not correspond to the expected behavior or turns out to be inappropriate in the given situation. At the same time, as a result of avoidance, the need to assert oneself increases.

Thus, the search for opportunity of self-affirmation begins in the substitution of natural activity with busyness, the demonstration of which promises recognition. In this busyness one learns to replace own true motives with rational, yet alien motives. Systematic destruction of spontaneous activity in the race after generally accepted, standardized life goals, causes a general reluctance to do anything. And the individual concludes that people are lazy by nature and do not want to do anything, unless motivated by material benefit or fear of punishment. Such a view encourages the use of corresponding educational methods.

Being busy is a choice. Daily tasks, projects, *deadlines* may not allow for a choice, but there is always freedom: to be addicted to doing and busyness, or to observe reflectively one's many activities. The ability to make such choices is awareness. Namely, it is about the balance between doing and realizing what has been done. Due to the limitation of information processing capacity, it is difficult to be fully aware of a very large amount of work to be done. Similarly, as eating too fast and too big of a meal causes problems for the belly to process it, too big amounts of work also cause problems to experience the activity. Reflexive observation often turns out to be problematic, and this also affects time in the learning process. Studies show that students overestimate the time they spend on various activities, including studying—they spend 1.25 times less time in classes than they think they do. At the same time if they overestimate the time spent on social networks by 1.5 times, then the time spent in electronic university study environment they overestimate even 2 times (Tanner et al., 2009).

4. "Purposefulness" in Transferring Living Time to Virtual Reality

To the extent that the goals of the learning process serve to strengthen the *ego* (a separate individuality that a person considers oneself to be), they cultivate anxiety. The *ego* feels itself as the doer, as the controller of the situation. The stronger a person resists real, i.e. ever-changing, and unpredictable life, the more they suffer. As an escape from the unpredictable and uncontrollable life, one can observe the ever-increasing transfer of one's time to virtual reality, based on the possibilities provided by TV, computers, phones, and tablets. This has also been facilitated by the period of the COVID-19 pandemic, in which individuals directly faced the inability to control their lives.

Technological advances in the field of rapid information exchange are undeniable. However, the abundance and speed of information does not allow us to stop and reflect on it. For example, it is now possible to obtain information via internet about various European universities to consider study opportunities in them in a very short time. However, networks do not provide an answer to the question: why should I study there? What significance does it bring to my life on what I'm going to learn there? IT connects everyone around the world but does not facilitate the individual to find contact with meaning.

The rapid expansion of information and communication technologies fully supports one's "purposefulness" as the pursuit of many small goals. It is difficult to find a daily task for which a mobile phone application has not yet been created. No wonder that a phone is nowadays not simply called a phone, but a smartphone. Thanks to these "smart" devices time is seemingly "freed up", for example, during one trip in public transport, one can answer to e-mails, communicate with friends, review photos, and listen to music. And doing almost all of it simultaneously. However, the pursuit of many small goals, even when the realization of these goals seems very simple, significantly reduces cognitive capacity and, therefore, the quality of these goals (Pashler, 1992).

The availability of many different forms of media is also a real challenge for the learning process in schools and universities. Nowadays pupils and students during their learning process like to confront themselves with different forms of media, often believing that they use their time more efficiently by doing two or more tasks simultaneously and not realizing that in this way they are sacrificing the quality of learning (Ellis et al., 2010). Research results indicate the association of simultaneous use of multiple forms of media with reduced cognitive control abilities (Ophir et al., 2009), lower academic achievement (Junco & Cotton, 2010), lower social well-being (Pea et al., 2012) and negative psychosocial effects such as depression and social anxiety (Becker et al., 2013). Regardless of individual personality traits, people who use a greater number of media devices at the same time have lower gray matter density in the frontal part of the cerebral cortex, which is responsible for the functions of human cognition and emotional control (Loh & Kanai, 2014).

The awareness of the finitude of time, which makes a person think that everything one does must be very fast and purposeful, also affects the ability to concentrate. In this regard, digital anxiety can be observed, when, for example, reading an interesting article on internet, one suddenly feels the urge to check an e-mail or send a photo on the phone—the internal "timer" seems to automatically switch one's attention to the next task, next achievable goal. It can also be explained as a kind of addiction to busyness—physiologically as a reward reaction for a "small victory", i.e. for achieving a goal, dopamine is released in the body, which encourages a person to strive for new goals in the digital environment (Berridge & Robinson, 1998).

5. Concept of Eternity in the Context of Learning

Modern person is usually indifferent to the idea of eternity, approaching it with positivist views and not seeing any practical application of it in the "real" everyday life. Wilber (2001) explains that the encounter with the eternal seems unrealistic because the meaning of the word "eternity" is mistakenly translated as a time span of millions and millions of years. However, if the word "eternity" refers not to some infinitely long period of time, but to a moment in which there is no time at all, it ceases to be a religious dogma or an exaggeration, and is practically experiential. These are moments in life that create a special exalted, mystical experience, and can occur not only when experiencing emergency situations or psychological crises, but also, for example, looking at a fabulously beautiful natural landscape, listening to deeply inspiring music or experiencing a very strong love. All these moments are united by the feeling of time stopping because the person is completely absorbed by the present moment. In addition, all of them are characterized by a sense of unified being, next to which the usual "reality" seems completely pale and insignificant. Ring (2012) defines such a moment of existence associated with an atypical state of consciousness as *omega experience*. Maslow (2022, Chapter 3) considers such moments as an essential aspect of one's self-actualization and calls them *peak experience*, noting that during it one's anxiety completely disappears. Moreover, such an existential experience is self-sufficient—it is not experienced as a means. People of different nationalities, religions and historical periods have described this type of experience similarly. Huxley (2022) has termed it "the perennial philosophy".

The above-mentioned experience of eternity brings significant changes in the cognitive process. Nature is revealed to the human being as something that exists by itself and for itself, and not as a "playground" created for one's needs. As Maslow (2022) points out, the experience of eternity or being unified gives the opportunity to free cognition from projecting its mercantile interests onto the subject—one becomes able to see nature in its personal unlimited existence, and not as something that must be used or from which to be afraid. In this way, for example, a virus can be viewed under an electron microscope as a delightful, awe-inspiring organization without dwelling on the threat it might pose.

However, such moments do not turn into regular experiences, because education, the purpose of which in our society is adaptation to external (physical and social) reality, limits the opportunities to experience them. Psychology, on the other hand, calls awareness of eternity an "altered state of consciousness", allying extroverted consciousness the norm, and considering *ego* separated from everything else as the true self.

In the learning process, the understanding of unified being is overshadowed by notions of divided time. As noted by Wittgenstein (2023), if by eternity we mean not an infinite span of time, but the absence of time, then the one who lives in the present lives forever. And even though eternity is right now, most people do not experience it that way. "Now" is experienced as something small, squeezed between the much larger "past" and "future", as something compressed and captive, and therefore fleeting. And what causes dissatisfaction and anxiety is always related to the past (mistakes, regret, guilt, etc.) or the future (fear of not realizing plans, failure). All one's valuable life goals are tied to the future. The fear of death makes one think all the time about the following day, set goals, make plans. In a similar way, the individual is attached to own past. One identifies oneself with own memories because they supposedly provide "knowledge". Also, the learning process is very often based on past feelings and events, that is, on what has been completed and is therefore easier to define and evaluate. Identifying with one's memories seems so obvious to many these days. Therefore, the *curriculum vitae* has acquired the status of an important document describing an individual. A person looks for hope and comfort in the future, while the past seems to guarantee the future—"if I existed yesterday, I will most likely exist also tomorrow". Kierkegaard (2021) connects such a division of time with one's alienation from oneself—the unhappy person is always absent from oneself, never present to oneself, but one can be absent, obviously, either in the past or in the future.

If memories are understood as the experience of the present moment, then the "memory folder" called "me" is also felt as one of the currently existing experiences, i.e. as an inseparable part of everything that exists now. Such an understanding of being present creates natural interest in the learning process that is not dependent on the limits of time. For example, the "breaking up" of the lesson in half a sentence (due to "lack of time") is not at all a defect if the participants were interested. Such incompleteness can serve as a mnemonic technique that facilitates memorizing and helps to retain the learned material in memory for a longer period. The moment of unexpectedness becomes acceptable both in one's own behavior and that of others, as well as in learning itself.

6. Conclusion

The problem of time relates to dissatisfaction and anxiety regarding the uncontrollable time, namely, the notion that time is supposedly divided into the past, the present and the future, as well as confusion in the face of death caused by a modern human's lack of experience of the whole existing unity.

The notion of the division of time is related to the notion of spatial division. Especially one can accentuate the relationship between the problem of time and the alienation of a person from oneself and own experience, which manifests as busyness, when learning serves only as means to correct past mistakes and achieve future goals, without being interested in the process itself. It points to the relevance of learning to be, which is possible only in the present.

Historically, man has sought and affirmed the experience of wholeness through faith in the absolute—God or some idealized leader, feeling own attachment to it. However, in the absence of it, a person would lose the foundation and need to go in search of oneself again. The problem is caused by the fact that the person does not realize the own situation and is not even interested in it. That is why attempts to restore one's unity with the world are relevant in pedagogical activity, realizing that a person, as a subject separated from it, suffers from a pronounced deficit of meaning. This does not mean that schools should teach "faith in anything", just to obtain some sense of belonging or security. It means learning not to avoid situations that provide the experience of wholeness, and accepting the absence of guarantees.

References

Baudrillard, J. (2012). *The ecstasy of communication*. Los Angeles: Semiotext(e).

Baudrillard, J. (2022). *Der symbolische Tausch und der Tod*. Berlin: Matthes & Seitz.

Becker, M. W., Alzahabi, R., & Hopwood, C. J. (2013). Media multitasking is associated with symptoms of depression and social anxiety. *Cyberpsychology, Behaviour and Social Networking*, 16, 132–135.

Berridge, K. C., & Robinson, T. E. (1998). What is the role of dopamine in reward: Hedonic impact, reward learning, or incentive salience? *Brain Research Reviews*, 28, 309–369.

Ellis, Y., Daniels, B. W., & Jauregui, A. (2010). The effect of multitasking on the grade performance of business students. *Research in Higher Education Journal*, 8, 1–11.

Erikson, E., Erikson, J., & Kivnick, H. (1994). *Vital involvement in old age*. New York: W. W. Norton & Company.

Feifel, H. (1977). *New meanings of death*. New York: McGraw-Hill.

Fromm, E. (2020). *To have or to be*. Greenwich: Upfront Books.

Garfield, C. (1975). Consciousness alteration and fear of death. *Journal of Transpersonal Psychology*, 7(2), 147–175.

Göhlich, M., & Zirfas, J. (2007). *Lernen: Ein pädagogischer Grundbegriff.* Stuttgart: W. Kohlhammer Verlag.

Heidegger, M. (2015). *Holzwege.* Frankfurt am Main: Verlag Vittorio Klostermann.

Heidegger, M. (2023). *Being and time.* Baden-Württemberg: Livraria Press.

Huxley, A. (2022). *The perennial philosophy.* New York: Legare Street Press.

Junco, R., & Cotton, S. R. (2010). Perceived academic effects of instant messaging use. *Computers and Education*, 56, 370–378.

Kierkegaard, S. (2021). *Either/or, Part I.* Macon: Mercer University Press.

Krishnamurti, J. (2020). *Freedom from the known.* Tamil Nadu: Krishnamurti Foundation India.

Lehman, H. C. (2017). *Age and achievement.* Princeton: Princeton University Press.

Loh, K. K., & Kanai, R. (2014). Higher media multi-tasking activity is associated with smaller gray-matter density in the anterior cingulate cortex. *PLoS ONE*, 9(9), Article e106698.

Maslow, A. H. (2022). *Toward a psychology of being.* Blacksburg: Wilder Publications.

Nietzsche, F. (2022). *Die fröhliche Wissenschaft.* München: Boer Verlag.

Ophir, E., Nass, C., & Wagner, A. D. (2009). Cognitive control in media multitaskers. *Proceedings of the National Academy of Sciences*, 106(33), 15583–15587.

Pashler, H. (1992). Attentional limitations in doing two tasks at the same time. *Current Directions in Psychological Science*, 1, 44–50.

Pea, R., Nass, C., Meheula, L., et al. (2012). Media use, face-to-face communication, media multitasking, and social well-being among 8- to 12-year-old girls. *Developmental Psychology*, 48, 327–336.

Plato. (2023). *Apology, crito, and phaedo of socrates.* Independently Published. ISBN: 9798388525161.

Ring, K. (2012). *Heading toward omega.* New York: Harper Perennial.

Schmid W. (2021) *Gelassenheit.* Berlin: Insel Verlag.

Tanner, J. R., Stewart, G., Maples, G. M., & Totaro, M. W. (2009). How business students spend their time—do they really know? *Research in Higher Education Journal*, 3, 76–84.

Vaillant, G. E. (2015). *Triumphs of experience: The men of the Harvard grant study.* Cambridge, MA: Belknap Press.

Veide, M. (2016). The understanding of life quality by students nowadays. *Rural Environment. Education. Personality*, 9, 187–194.

Wilber, K. (2001). *No boundary: Eastern and Western approaches to personal growth*. Boston: Shambhala.

Wittgenstein, L. (2023). *Tractatus logico-philosophicus*. Oxford: Oxford University Press.

Yalom, I. (2020). *Existential psychotherapy*. New York: Basic Books.

Yalom, I. (2022). *Staring at the sun*. San Francisco: Jossey-Bass.

www.ingramcontent.com/pod-product-compliance
Ingram Content Group UK Ltd.
Pitfield, Milton Keynes, MK11 3LW, UK
UKHW021014120926
8556IPUK00040B/1144

9 783631 919248